In the Life of
a Romany Gypsy

IN THE LIFE OF A ROMANY GYPSY

Manfri Frederick Wood

Edited by John A. Brune

Illustrated by Andrew Young

Routledge & Kegan Paul
London and Boston

First published 1973
by Routledge & Kegan Paul Ltd
Broadway House, 68-74 Carter Lane,
London EC4V 5EL and
9 Park Street,
Boston, Mass. 02108, U.S.A.

Printed in Great Britain by
Alden & Mowbray Ltd
at the Alden Press, Oxford

ISBN 0 7100 7595 2

Contents

Introduction

I only had about two years in primary school and that was my lot. In the second year they taught me to read and write and that was a very useful bit of knowledge. Writing has always been a very difficult occupation for me, and spelling was something I never got the hang of, so, if anybody had told me years ago that one day I would sit down to write a book I would have laughed at him.

But I am a very fluent reader, and whenever I see a book anywhere that is supposed to be on the Gypsy way of life, or on Gypsy traditions, I borrow it. Every book on Gypsies that I have ever read through was either for the most part nonsense, or else a very good Didikai book. With the exception of one excellent, thick, and rather expensive book by John Sampson on the dialect of the Gypsies of Wales—which makes very difficult reading—there was not a single Romany book around as far as I could see. So one day I decided to fill the gap and write this book myself.

After I had written about half of my book I showed it to John Brune, who did not think that any publisher today would look at it as it was in my handwriting and spelling. He also found it somewhat disorganized. He offered to rearrange my script and to edit it while still preserving the style in which it was written. I gladly accepted his offer and kept supplying him with the rest of the material over a period of a few months. The present book is the result. His work is gratefully acknowledged.

I hope that this book will clear up at least some of the misunderstandings that exist to this day between my people and the Gorgios.

A Branch of the Tree
of the Woods

I am a Romany. I come from one of the oldest Romany families in Britain. My branch of the tribe was always a family of carpenters, joiners, wagon-builders, wheelwrights, wood-carvers and horse-dealers.

We were not always called Wood. A few hundred years ago the tribe was called Akbar. They were settled in Turkey and they travelled both in Turkey and Greece. In time there were too many of them for comfort and so they drew lots to decide who was to stay on in that part of the world and who was to move on. Then some of them moved north into the Russian and Tartar lands and the rest went north and west through the length and breadth of Europe. One party of about eighty drifted into France with some forged documents that gave them a free passage wherever they went. This was supposed to be from the Pope. They pretended to be Christian fugitives from Egypt and their head man claimed to be the deposed king of Little Egypt. Akbar was not a good name to run around with in Europe at the time as it sounded too Mohammedan—so they changed their name to Hator; but that did not really help much as at that time they lived mainly on fraud and fortune telling, robbery with violence, and extortion. Sometimes when they got to the walls of a city they were paid to go away, other times there was a battle—and if they lost and some of them were taken prisoner, they were beaten to death or burnt at the stake.

This was the time of the Wars of the Roses. France was getting too hot for the Hators, so they sent scouts over the English Channel to find out the lie of the land. One of them ran into an army of Lancastrians with Queen Margaret at their head

I

going towards London from Wakefield in Yorkshire. When they stopped for a short break the Queen made the scout out a free pass for the whole tribe in return for a promise of support of the Lancastrians against the Yorkists. A boat was also arranged. This got the tribe into the country, but not long after they arrived the Queen had to flee to France and the Hators forgot about York and Lancaster because they had problems of their own. They first went to Epping Forest, then to New Forest. Then they divided the country into Romany territories and split up. The main tribe kept the name Hator but all the others changed over to English names like Locke, Boswell, Wood, and so forth. The Woods took on the name because they were good craftsmen in wood; they were also musicians. But whatever skills they had, they still made their living mainly by highway robbery and fortune-telling.

When the last of the Hators died—Giles Hator—the various tribes parted company. Some of them have only married within their own family ever since. Most of the others had more sense and frequently mixed their blood with other families.

The Woods made a point of accepting the occasional Gorgio into the tribe—but it had to be a very special type of Gorgio that fitted well into the Romany way of life. If any of them fell foul with the rest of the tribe, or married someone the chief of the tribe did not approve of, they were cast out as renegades; and once out they were never taken back into the tribe. If they had been very popular until they were cast out, it was reckoned that they died on the day they were cast out—but they were still remembered; but if they were hot-heads and not really liked at any time they were either forgotten or counted as born dead or remembered as people who died young. They had to be very careful to keep out of the sight of the tribe from the day after they were cast out.

As I said before, until about 300 years ago most of the Gypsies in this country lived on fraud, fortune-telling and highway robbery. Not many of the Woods were caught—but four or five of them were executed for highway robbery at Gloucester about 250 years ago. Two half-brothers, Abraham and John, were the last of the regular highwaymen in the tribe and they were both hanged together. Abraham's son, Bohemia, took to religion and was baptized at Selattyn, and until recently there was a document dated 1715 that proved it—but this was burned in the last war. His other son, Lucas, took to religion about the same time—but he had been married to a Gorgio woman for about twenty years before he did so. They had only one child, a daughter they called Sarah, after the Saint Sarah, the black virgin of the Romanies. She was born about 1695 at Bala or Corwen in North Wales. Bohemia's son, Abram, was born about four years later near Frome in Somerset. He moved into Wales as a young man and married Sarah. They were both very strictly religious. They settled in North Wales and did not travel a lot. All the Woods of Wales are descended from Abram and Sarah.

Abram Wood was the first Romany of the tribe who made an honest living, mainly as a musician. He was the man who introduced the fiddle into Wales. He was also a harper and he taught all of his children to make music; and they could all read and write too. He had three sons and one daughter. His oldest son, Valentine, married Jane Boswell; William married Mary Stanley; Solomon married a Gorgio, Jane Hughes; and Demaris married Meredith Ingram. So in this generation there was all new blood—and this is how the tribe kept healthy. We are now reaching into the last century—Abram died in 1799 and lies buried at Llangelynin; Valentine died in 1818 aged about seventy-five.

Most of these things were never written down except in the family Bibles which were from time to time replaced. Dates never meant much to Romanies so there are very few that we remember. But there are landmarks from which we could work out within a year or two when any of the things I mentioned happened. There must be a record somewhere that gives the date when Queen Margaret led an army from Wakefield to London, and from that one might be able to trace a copy of the free passage she gave to the Hators. From that you could work out roughly how many generations it was before Abram married Sarah. I suppose, until quite recently, everybody descended from Abram and Sarah remembered how their own family fitted into the jigsaw—what you would call the family tree—which must by now be eight or nine generations removed from Abram Wood. In the beginning of this century the last link with the second generation of the tribe of Abram Wood was Saiforella Wood, also called Mary or Taw, who was for many years the chief of the tribe. She was the granddaughter of Valentine Wood and was born about ten years after Abram Wood died. Until her own death in 1905 she walked the hills visiting all the hundreds of blood relations to keep the old ties firm and to pass on all the news. She regularly visited every grave of any member of the tribe buried in Wales, Gloucestershire and Shropshire; and she even kept contact with some who had been cast out by the rest of the tribe for becoming too much like ordinary house-dwellers. She was said to be one of the best story-tellers in the old grammatical Romany language, and she could recall every single member of the tribe that had not been cast out from Abram and Sarah right on to the new generation at the turn of the century—and there were hundreds of names!

Through her we all still remember the third generation of Woods and Ingrams—but after that we only remember our own lines and the few families that became famous for one reason or another—like the Woods of Bala and Corwen, the Roberts who were harpers to Queen Victoria, and some of the Ingrams.

Now Valentine Wood married Jane Boswell and they had five children. The first two married Gorgios; they were called Adam and Alabaina. Some of Alabaina's descendants are married into the Lee and Jones tribes but they are mainly city people now. The third son, married his first cousin, Silvaina, who was the daughter of Abram and Sarah's second son, William Wood, and Mary Stanley. For this they had to pretend that they were second cousins. Valentine's fourth child, Jeremiah, married Ann Griffiths, a Gorgio. His fifth child was a daughter, Ellen—called 'Black Ellen' or 'Blind Nellie'. She married her first cousin, William, who was the son of Abram Wood's third son, Solomon, and Jane Hughes. So there were two sets of first cousins married into that generation. Abram Wood had twenty grandchildren, of whom three were Ingrams. He was dead before most of them were born. About half of them married Gorgios, but most of them remained Romanies and so did their children; the particular Gorgios they married were acceptable to the tribe. But Romany or not, the Woods in Wales travelled a good deal less than did the Romanies elsewhere. Wales is an ideal country for living a natural life provided you know how to earn your money there. So the arguments against settling down more or less in one place are not so great for a Welsh Gypsy as they would be for the same man in England.

Now the next generation ran to about sixty people who died towards the end of the last century and the beginning of this present century. Thomas and Silvaina had a family of twelve. One of them really died when she was very young; the twelfth one was a son called Frederick who fell out with the rest of them—partly in a dispute over land, over some horse deals, and over a religious squabble that most people would laugh at nowadays. He was cast out and never to be mentioned again but somehow they never got a chance to forget him because he did not go all that quietly. Their seventh child was a daughter, Saiforella, or Taw, who was the chief of the tribe for many years, as I mentioned before. She married her cousin, Black Henry, who was the son of her grandfather's fifth child, Ellen, and her first cousin, William. Saiforella had two children before she married Black Henry. Then she and Henry had seven more. The most famous among them was Matthew Wood who was a great story-teller and one of the last people to speak in the pure deep Romany tongue in this country. He was a great friend of Augustus John, the painter, and Nansi Richard-Jones, the triple-harpist. He was one of the main sources for John Sampson, who put together a thick book on Welsh Romany and another of Welsh Gypsy folk tales. This John Sampson, incidently, was the only Gorgio ever to be accepted as a full Romany in this country by all the Romanies in the West Country and Wales. At least I have never heard of another Gorgio to be accepted in this way; and when he died he was given a full traditional Romany cremation with all the main members of the Welsh Romany tribes taking part.

Matthew married Llwyddan Wood who was the daughter of Edmund and Eliza Wood; Edmund was the son of Black Ellen and William; and Eliza was the daughter of Jeremiah Wood and Ann Griffiths. So the family was very closely intermarried at this stage.

Matthew had five children, four sons and one daughter. They were Henry, who was also called Turpin, Mary, who died of lockjaw at the age of six, Manfri, Howell and Jim. Howell never married; the other three all married Gorgios. They were the last three really good speakers of the pure deep Romany language of Wales. Howell is remembered mainly for his step dancing. They are all dead now. Manfri and Howell lie buried in adjoining graves in a churchyard by the lake near Bala in Merioneth. If you jumped over the wall into the next section of the cemetery from Manfri's grave, you would land on the grave of Matthew.

Manfri lived in Bala for the greater part of his life. He was not a poacher—he didn't have to be—he was a gamekeeper. He and his wife, Jane Yates, owned a small house and he was known as 'the fisherman on the lake'. He had one son and two daughters. His son, James, moved to London. His eldest daughter, Alice, married a local stone-mason, a rugged outdoor type, Norman Davies, and they have three children—one son and two daughters. Alice looks like a pure Romany with not a trace of Gorgio blood in her, but her children already look like all the other local kids—Welsh. They are less than a quarter Romany by blood. Manfri's third child, Sarah Elizabeth, married a local journalist. Manfri's elder brother, Henry, or Turpin Wood, was a wild man who married Myfanwy Hughes. He had one daughter and two sons. They were called Violet May, Jim (Turpin the Second) and Robert John. Jim Wood married Ellen Tizzard and had a son called William.

Now the Woods of Bala are the nearest branch of the tribe to my own family. My grandfather, Frederick, who was the twelfth child of Thomas and Silvaina Wood was born about 1830. He was not the first Frederick in the tribe, though he was the first of that name in the Welsh branch of the Woods. The first Frederick in the tribe was the son of Ebenezer Wood, who was a son or a grandson of the highwayman, John Wood. Ebenezer had a row with his wife Hannah, gave her a good hiding and then walked out on her and went over the water to fight for Frederick the Great of Prussia in his Silesian war. Ebenezer was killed in a place called Torgau just a few months later and when the news came to Hannah Wood she was in labour. She had a son and called him Frederick after the king of Prussia whom Ebenezer had died for. This Frederick was an exceptionally good man who never had a quarrel with anyone and he was well liked by the Romanies both in England and Wales, and Thomas and Silvaina were particularly fond of his company. So when their last son, my grandfather, was born, and they just heard that this Frederick Wood had died, they called their baby Frederick after him.

2   A Bit of the Old Life

When my grandfather fell out with the rest of the Welsh family—
who in his opinion were gradually turning into Gorgios anyway—
he decided to go back to a more Romany way of life himself.
To do this he went over to Hampshire where some of the
English branch of the tribe were travelling in a circle at the
time, and there he married my grandmother, Eliza, who for
many years, as far back as I can remember, was the chief of the
tribe. In those days we always travelled as a tribe—there were
always thirty-five to forty wagons and loads of dogs, horses,
ferrets and domestic fowls as well as song-birds on the road
with us. We were a big tribe—many uncles and aunts—each
wagon was a family—and granduncles, grandaunts, cousins,
brothers and sisters—always stopping and moving on together in
a bunch. Nothing quite like it has been seen on the roads of
England for a good many years now.

There would be very little point in trying to recall
all of the people in the tribe when I was young. I had dealings with
only a handful of them; of course, when I was a toddler, I
played around with all the other toddlers, but as soon as I was
old enough to do a job of work, all my time was spent with the
people I worked with—and we just got on with our work and
never became too intimate. The nearest people to me were my
grandparents, my parents and one of my uncles—so I will introduce them now, and then just tell things as they come to my mind.

Now my father's name was always Frederick or
Long Fred. My favourite uncle's name was Jerry—that's what
we would have called him, though sometimes we called him
Jeremiah—but that wasn't his real name; his name was Frederick

as well. It would have been inconvenient to call him Frederick and that's why he became Jerry. But my grandfather used to use three names apart from Frederick, which he dropped when he left Wales. I've known him to be called Thomas, I've known him to be called Elfrid and I've also known him to be called George. In some places my mother's name was Florence, in others she was called Bertha and there were lots of places where she was known as Annie and in other places again she was called Flo. And that's as far as I intend to go with my family tree.

My father was one of the real old-fashioned Romanies. He believed in the old Romany traditions. His clothes had to be made in the old Romany way. His trousers were always of the stovepipe-leg type with six rows of stitching round the bottom, flap fronts, and pipe seams at the sides. He always wore a shirt made in the old true style of the Romany; he always wore a handkerchief round his neck printed to a certain pattern; he always wore a leather waistcoat to work in and a very heavily embroidered waistcoat for dress. He was a man who took a pride in everything he had and everything he owned. He also took a great pride in his work. His clothes were absolutely spotless—he was spotless in appearance in every way, and he was a man that was very strict as well as being smart; his horses, his harness, his wagons, trolleys and carts were a credit to him. His carts, wagons and trolleys were always freshly varnished every year and the brasswork on them always shone like gold; the trace-chain on his harness always shone like silver; the brass buckles always shone like gold; the black leather harness round the collar and everywhere else always shone like patent—also his skeleton harness, his brown patent skeleton harness always shone. He was a man who was always respected wherever he went; he could always see things in a horse that nobody else could see; he was a very clever man at operating on horses; he was a very clever man in his selection of a horse.

My father didn't believe in anything that was mechanical in any way. He would not even put a shilling in a gas meter; he would not even screw a connector on a bike; everything in his way had to be done with horses or other animals— nothing mechanical whatsoever. He was a man who would not be beaten by anybody; if spoken to properly he would answer you—but if he was spoken to sharply or in an impolite way he would not answer you—and he would not answer you until you spoke to him in a proper way. And if you insulted him you would remember the lesson he taught you for the rest of your life; for he was the sort of man that if he came to a fight the only way that you could beat him was that you would practically have to kill him stone dead. If it meant a fight with some other man and it meant a true fair fight, he would have to be an exceptionally strong man to beat my father because my father was as strong as a horse and of a very heavy build. He was in fact beaten, but only on a very few occasions. Now, if he stood up to a man to fight and the man beat him by fair means, that was all right—they'd shake hands and go for a drink, and he'd always be the best of friends with him; but if ever it came to a fight with anybody over a deal, or over him letting a pony and trolley out on hire, like he had done in the past, and there had been a fight when he went to collect the rents for the hire of that trolley and harness—if the man done him dirty in that fight—if he used a foul of any sort—that man regretted the day he was born because my father would cripple him.

My father was a great stickler for rules, but he always said that the rules don't apply to anybody who breaks them and that only a fool observes the rules with somebody who doesn't observe them as well.

He was a man that knew all the tricks of the trade. When he went into a sale—whether it was a horse sale, or a farm auction—he didn't have to look round to see what was at the right-hand side or what was at the left-hand side of him. If he was looking at the auctioneer he knew exactly what was there, he'd see everything in one go, and everything registered. He knew who was on the left-hand side, who was on the right, he knew exactly what they were doing and he knew who was behind him and what was going on. He was exceptionally observant in every way; when a horse was being run up and down in a sale, he would watch that horse, he would watch the way the horse turned to see the functioning of its muscles in the shoulders; he would watch the action in the stifle in the hind-

quarters and see the way the horse carried its head—also he'd look how the horse moved its tail; by watching all these things my father could tell if a horse had been loaded, doctored in some way or temporarily levelled up for the purpose of the sale. These things only a horse dealer and men in the horse trade understand.

My father was a very clever man with the breaking in of horses to work; he was very good in controlling horses in traffic; he could talk horses and dogs into doing things; he didn't believe in cruelty at all to animals. He'd never hit a horse with a whip unless it was downright necessary. He'd train a horse in a way that a lot of men would never have the patience to do. I've seen my father with a 'nappy horse'—what we'd call a 'nappy horse' or a 'bouncer' that other people have handled and they couldn't do any good with—and I've seen him just talking to this horse in his way and make it tremble and shake and come out into a white sweat lather, just by talking alone, and when he said 'go' that horse went, and when he said 'stop' it stopped.

He was a very clever man with the curing of horses from different illnesses; but he always believed in the old way. If a horse had an abscess, he didn't believe in prolonging anything— he believed in getting out the knife and cutting it out. I've never known my father ever lose a horse over an operation he has performed. He's performed operations on horses that the Blue Cross Hospital—the Veterinary Hospital at New Cross in south-east London—had turned down; I've seen him take warts off a horse's tummy that other veterinary surgeons with a diploma would not have attempted to do. His operations were always a great success.

My father was always a man of very few words; he had no sense of humour at all; he always believed in coming to the point straight away; he never did believe in a person saying things to him in a round-about way. He wanted things said out straight away and to the point—always liked his cards on the table.

My father was a man that only told anybody to do anything once; if he wanted something shifted that was in front of his yard—for instance, if anybody parked a motor car in front of the yard and he couldn't get out, or nobody could get in— he'd tell them to shift it at once and he would also tell them what he would do if they put it there again—and if they put it there again, he'd do it—he'd up with a sledgehammer and he'd smash it; and he'd take the consequences afterwards. He was feared and respected by everybody wherever he went because he was a man of his word, and that was his bond, and he expected everybody to be the same way. The people who had done my father wrong feared him, and the people who had dealt with my father on business always respected him. He was always a fair man in dealing—he never caught anybody with a horse— if he had a horse to sell and the horse did have something wrong with it, which wasn't very often, he'd always tell the person that wanted to buy it what was wrong with that horse. He always thought of a future sale. He never thought of just that time and of that particular moment—he always thought of what was going to happen in the future. If he was going to sell a horse to somebody he always thought that if he was fair to these people they would some day want a sale from him again; and in return for always treating his customers fairly he expected fair treatment from them. So if he had a horse of a certain type he knew exactly where he could take it to make a sale.

We used to travel all over Surrey, all over Essex and Hampshire, up into Oxfordshire, over to Wales, back into Gloucestershire—we did quite a lot of travelling during the months we were a-travelling—and these different places we went to—whether it was a horse sale in Kent, or a horse sale in Surrey, whether it was Barnet or Barbican, or whether we went to the mineheads in Wales or whether we went to the Curragh in Ireland, he knew exactly what he was looking for and he knew who the person would be that he was going to make this horse a sale to. Whether it was a big draught horse—a shire horse—or whether it was a forest pony, or whether it was a hack—he knew exactly where to dispose of this horse; and there were times when we were away in Kent during the fruit-picking season when gentlemen have come up by train or car, and asked to see my father about a certain particular type of horse; they might be looking for a horse of a certain colour and height, of a certain age, training or temperament; and they wanted to know whether he knew where he could pick up such a horse for them. Sometimes he would have the horse they were looking for right on the spot; but if he did not know at the particular time where he could go and purchase a horse like that, he would tell that man that he would get him the horse he needed and on our travels he would find this horse.

On one particular occasion we were stopping in a place just outside Hastings,—a place called Battle—we were apple-picking and a gentleman came all the way from Gloucester to see my father specially, as he wanted a big black shire horse with four white feet and a white blaze, and he asked my father if he knew where there was such a horse, and my father said he did— he had one tied to the hedge at that very moment. He took the gentleman and showed him the horse, and the gentleman wanted to buy the horse there and then—but my father said that he could not have the horse just yet as it had not been broken in; it was only a colt. The gentleman asked if he could buy it when it was broken in and my father said that he would sell it to him but that he could not tell him for how much until he got it to Gloucester later in the year. He said that we would break the horse in, we would send word when we were coming, and when we got to Gloucester he could have a veterinary surgeon there to look the horse over and they would have a deal.

The next day my father asked the farmer on the farm next to where we were picking the apples whether he could borrow the plough to break this horse in—and the farmer agreed to let him have it on certain conditions. My father always broke the big draught horses in behind the plough, as a draught horse was always best broken in on soft ground. If a draught horse was broken in on soft ground and he had a load up and he felt the load behind him, particularly if the ground was a little bit wet, he'd draw. But if he was broken in on hard ground—as a lot of these heavy horses are—they wouldn't draw at all as soon as they felt the weight. Broken in behind the plough was different altogether. My father never did it any other way. This rarely took more than three days and sometimes it only took two.

The next day my father put this horse beside a wagon horse, which was another big horse, and he started him on the plough; and by four o'clock in the afternoon the horse was almost broken in. It only meant after that starting to break in the horse to traffic. Breaking in this horse to traffic was one of my jobs. My father was on the trolley, the horse was harnessed to the trolley and I was at the horse's head. We went along the roads and country lanes into the busiest streets in the various country towns round and about and all the time we were in the towns it was my job to hold the bridle of the horse. But all I had to do was hold the bridle. The horse had to answer to the reins and to my father's words. We did have a few minor accidents at times when breaking in various horses to traffic, but this particular horse came to it like a swan to a river. Traffic didn't seem to worry it at all and it picked up my father's words and signs like a baby—when he told him to stop and told him to turn, he stopped and he turned.

After the apple-picking was finished on this particular farm we started to make our way up into Gloucestershire. We drove this horse to Gloucestershire—we drove him with a heavy wagon behind him and when we got to Gloucestershire we found this man. He knew we were coming and what day we were going to arrive, as a cable had been sent through the post. This gentleman did not bother to have a veterinary surgeon—he knew that this horse would be perfect in every way. We pulled onto this gentleman's land, and before we left his farm my father showed him the way this horse could work the side of the pole, single-handed or behind a plough; and that horse turned out to be one of the finest ploughing horses that gentleman had ever purchased.

Now about my uncle Jerry and my grandfather—they could handle horses and dogs as well as any of the rest of the tribe, though perhaps not quite in my father's class, but in addition they were also woodworkers. It was from them that I learned carpentry, joinery, wood-carving and making wheels. I don't think there was anything they couldn't do in wood, and when they did a job they did it perfect in every way.

Their motto was, 'There's only one way to do a

job, and that is the right way.' It never once occurred to them that there might be a better way of doing one or the other job; the right way was well tried, experiments are wasteful and materials are expensive—and as the right way gave you a perfect article that would last for many years and looked good, and any other way they knew of was shoddy-looking and didn't last, they always insisted on doing their work the right way—and this is how they kept all their customers for life. What is more, they never attempted to do a job unless they knew how to do it in the right way.

It didn't matter what job my grandfather tackled, whether it was outside woodwork; whether it was a metal job; or whether it was cutting or splicing of harness—or making a pair of shoes—he did this in the way it should be done. He could drill and rivet china—valuable china—without batting an eyebrow; he could mend all different kinds of metal objects that used to melt when they got hot; he was a man that could solder aluminium—he invented the solder himself—nobody would bother with anything like that nowadays, but in those days it was still thought worth doing this.

He knew a certain amount of chemistry; he could remove tattoo without a skin graft. For this he first painted over the skin with a concentrated solution of tannin—all over the tattoos that had to be removed. He then put a fine needle in boiling water and pricked it into the tattoo design—this was a fine series of needle pricks all over the design that was to be removed. Over the top of this pricked design he made a coat of nitrate of silver. This coat or layer gradually soaks into the needle pricks and you can see it spread into the upper layers of the skin surrounding the tattoo design. For the next four days this skin layer with the combined tannin and silver nitrate in it was regularly powdered with tannin. Eventually the pricked parts turned black and formed a thin crust which after two or three weeks scabbed off. After this, all that remained to see for a few months was an inflammation that was quite painless and didn't itch; this wore off after five or six weeks if you treated it with hedgehog oil; otherwise it would persist for many months before you got rid of it. This sort of operation could only be performed by a careful person with a steady hand—and he had to be a clean operator or his patient would end up with an infection that might finish him off.

My grandfather was also a good toolmaker. Until recently I still used a plane made by him—but even the best tools wear in time if you use them constantly and so I finally had to throw it out and make myself a new plane of the same design. He always used to sharpen different kinds of instruments and tools—perfectly and in exactly the way they should be done. He could sharpen a cut-throat razor on an oilstone when it could no longer be stropped, when another man would have to send it away to be ground in a shop. He sharpened knives, sickles, scythes and axes, various modern types of grass-cutting implements, so that people came back to him when the job needed to be done again;—sheep-shearing shears he'd sharpen by hand —and garden shears and scissors—which a lot of the travelling knife-grinders ruin—he would do them all in the proper professional way. He was a man who always took pride in what he was doing. If a toecap on a pair of boots needed replacing, he could take that toecap off, and he'd sit on the ground with a piece of leather and his cobbling implements and he would make a new toecap out of that piece of leather and he would put it on that boot. Nothing was ever wasted with him unless it was altogether beyond repair. I don't think he was ever beaten by a job in his life.

My grandfather was in many ways a hard man like my father but he was a different type of man in lots of ways; like my father he liked anybody to come to the point—but he wasn't like my father in many ways. If he could talk his way out of trouble he would, but if there was trouble he never ran away. My father was a different man altogether in this way—if anybody came to him with trouble on his lips straight away, he found trouble straight away—but not my grandfather—he'd try and talk his way out. Getting through his work and business deals smoothly and without any unnecessary complications was much more important to him than any minor dispute with whatever damned fool happened to cross his path. When we were building a wagon and we were doing the carving on a wagon, or doing the butterflies on the wagon, he would first show us very patiently the way to do this job; he taught us the way to hold our tools and the way to sharpen them, and while we were at work on that wagon, my grandfather or one of my uncles, usually uncle Jerry, would watch over us. Oh yes, by God, and didn't they just watch over you! They would watch over you—and if you went wrong somewhere they would put you right; and if you went wrong for a second time they would put you right again; but if you went wrong for a third time—woe betide you! They just wouldn't say, 'You've done that wrong'—they'd hit you and knock you down, and when you got up and you started again and you went wrong again, they'd knock you down again—they were very hard people in every way. And they would take no nonsense from any outsider. If anybody from outside did any serious injury to any of us that would have to be paid for in kind; if it was serious enough the whole tribe would be involved in the revenge.

When I was of school age, my cousin—the oldest girl at the time—was fourteen years old. We were camped in a place in Kent. My cousin was left to look after the smaller children while the women went out calling and the men were at a horse market. My cousin took the small children for a walk up the lane and got them to pick some bluebells in the wood. While they were picking bluebells a man appeared out of the wood and he asked my cousin was she on her own and were there any grown-ups with her. When she told the man she was the oldest one there, looking after the children, he knocked her down and ripped her dress and underclothes off; she pleaded with the man not to abuse her but she was raped while the other children screamed their heads off for help—but nobody came to her aid.

It took her some time to get back to the camp and when my mother and aunts got back she was in such a shocked state she could not speak. When the men came back from the horse market they searched all the area and all the pubs but could not find a man that fitted her description of the man that had raped her.

It was more than ten years after this that she recognized this man in Maidstone Market. She told my aunt and my aunt told my uncle and he told all the rest of the tribe that the man was there at the market—and two of them shadowed him to make sure he wouldn't get away until everybody had been alerted for the showdown. Then my uncle and my father went to the man and dragged him to where my cousin stood to make sure there was no mistake as to his identity. When my cousin confronted him he pleaded with my uncle not to send for the police. My uncle told him that he had no intention of sending for the police as this had to be done in the Romany way. My uncle then went for him with his horse-whip. As the man turned to run the other way my father went for him with his horse-whip. He turned in another direction where one of my cousins horse-whipped him—and it didn't matter which way he turned but he found himself confronted by one of my relations who knew how to handle a horse-whip. He could not get out of the ring nor could he get a blow in edgeways himself and he was beaten to an inch of his life before the police got there to break it up. They told the man they would beat him every time they met him again—once he was crossing a bridge on crutches when they threw him into the river and he damned near drowned—and they told him they would make him suffer twice over for every nightmare that my cousin had suffered over his outrage.

Well, this wasn't the end of the story by any means. They made sure they didn't murder him as it wasn't worth swinging for it—but every time they met him again they were had up for assault and bodily harm. He was crippled for life and he was never safe again until he finally left the country altogether.

I remember another time when the tribe was up in arms—this time against a local G.P.—but only for one night. I was in my early teens. It was Derby week on Epsom Downs and one of my aunts was in labour. After some hours my mother and my grandmother realized there was an obstruction and they sent me on a push-bike in the early hours of the morning to fetch a doctor.

I rode to the doctor's house and knocked at the door continuously for several minutes until the doctor's wife opened an upstairs window and asked what was wrong. I asked her to come down to the front door so I could explain. She came down, I explained the situation and she went upstairs to wake the doctor and see if he would come to see my aunt. He came downstairs but as soon as he saw me he told me to be off as he had no time for Gypsies.

I rode back as fast as I could to where we camped and told my father what had happened. He rounded up all my uncles and they went on horseback and with a pony and trap to the doctor's house, broke down the front door, went upstairs and pulled the doctor out of bed. They told him that they needed his help and were not going to take no for an answer. They ripped out the telephone and told the doctor to slip on his dressing gown over his nightshirt as they couldn't wait at this stage for him to make himself decent. They went with him to the surgery to get the black bag and then they drove him in the pony and trap to Epsom Downs. When they got to where we were a-camping, my uncle said to the doctor, 'You see this big bough of this here oak-tree? If anything happens to my monashay on account of your delay in coming here, you'll be swinging from it before this night is out.'

The doctor did not look like a happy man to me and he seemed to have the shakes—not at all like my father when he was about to operate on a horse—but at this stage there would not have been enough time to find another doctor who was more sure of himself and not unhappy.

The doctor was surprised what a good clean bed my aunt was lying in and he remarked on it. He got to work with my mother and my aunt to deliver the child and everything went well. My uncle then paid the doctor a fee and he was driven back in the pony and trap. The next day we expected the police to call with half a dozen charges connected with abducting the doctor for a few hours—but the doctor never contacted the police at all. So that was the end of it except that from then on the doctor would then see any of my family and relatives at any time of the day or night.

Another bit of quick retribution I remember occurred when I was about twelve years of age and we had just got back into the yard at the end of the autumn. One day a man came along and knocked at the door of the wagon and he told my mother that he was a school officer and we would all have to go to school. A few days after, my mother took me and my cousins to school and from then on for a few days my different aunts took turns in taking all of us to school and after that we had to make our own way there. The teachers humiliated us like a lot of monkeys in the zoo and made us feel uncomfortable before the whole class—just because we were Gypsies and a bit different from the rest. Every time something was done inside the school or after school we were the ones that got the blame. My cousins and I could not read or write and we were not actually helped to learn either, at this stage of our schooling. All the teachers seemed to want with us was an excuse to give us the cane. The only lessons I was good at at school were woodwork, metalwork and singing, and in these I always got top marks.

On one particular occasion I was in a metalwork class making a picture hook, when some prank or other had been played in the school, and the headmaster came straight to the metalwork room—as my cousins and myself were the first that came to his mind. As the headmaster walked through the metalwork-room door, on his left in the corner stood some metal tubing. He picked up one of these metal tubes and I had my back to him, and being as I was the nearest, he made straight for me. He upped with the metal tube and swiped me at the back of my neck. I was out for the count—in fact I am lucky I wasn't killed or crippled for life over this. When I went home to dinner that day and I sat down to eat, my father grabbed me and told me to wash my neck. I went and washed my neck and sat down again to have my dinner. My father jumped up again and dragged me away in order to scrub my neck when he noticed that I had a stiff neck and a job to move my head—and he could see that my neck wasn't dirty but it was all blue. He asked me how it happened and I told him. So he came back to school with me after dinner.

We went straight through to the headmaster's room and he barged in without knocking, pulling me in with him. He asked the headmaster if it was true that he had hit me on the back of the neck with a metal tube and when the headmaster agreed that he had, my father bent forward and grabbed him by his tie and his shirtfront and pulled him towards him. He hit him hard in the face and he told him that it would have been alright if he had tanned my arse with a cane if I had really done anything wrong but apart from that if I wanted hitting he could do all the hitting himself and did not need any headmaster to do it for him. He then pulled the headmaster out in the corridor and set about him with the horse-whip. I can't recall if my father was charged with assault for this—he probably was—but from that day on school became a good deal more bearable for all of us; we were never manhandled again and they actually began teaching us education, as the saying goes when Gypsies talk of 'the three Rs'.

Another time when an old score had to be settled—this concerns my uncle Jerry—there was no violence involved at all. I remember some years before the war there was a butcher my uncle had dealings with who would not pay up the money he owed, and my uncle told the butcher that he would have his own back if it took him all his life and he said he would wait until the right opportunity occurred. Now a few years after the war when food was still rationed this particular butcher heard that my uncle had got quite a few geese, and as Christmas was coming on he came to see my uncle. My uncle told the butcher that he had more geese than he actually had, and he also told him that he was waiting for some more to come in. The butcher asked my uncle would he sell him these geese—so many live birds and so many dead—and my uncle said he would sell him the lot for cash on delivery.

Now, since Christmas was so near, my uncle got me to help him feed some very old swans on a near-by gravel pit for several weeks running—and about three days before the deal with the butcher we went to the gravel pit and caught several of these swans—though not as many as we would have liked. I then helped my uncle kill and prepare the geese for the sale.

We took the geese and the swans to the butcher in the dark—and the live birds of course were mainly the swans which we sold to the butcher for geese. For transporting these live birds we had to use some wicker poultry cages. Well, a goose sticks her head out at one end and there is no opening at the other end at all for the tail feathers to stick out. All the baskets that had geese in them had a goose's head sticking out of the opening, but the swans had their tail feathers sticking out instead. After my uncle had pocketed the money, we let the live birds loose one by one into the butcher's barn and he locked up. As the deal was done outside in the dark, the butcher could not see the fiddle and he paid my uncle out before the live birds were released.

The next morning when the butcher opened his barn he found a lot of swans among his geese. He came straight over to have it out with my uncle. My uncle asked the butcher if he remembered how he had done him before the war; and he told him that this was the way of getting his own back. The butcher told him that he thought my uncle had forgotten all about this, and my uncle said that a Romany never forgets a bad deal and that he will always get his own back on people who pull tricks on him. The butcher said he was going to the police and my uncle said he could do so if he liked as the whole deal was against the law anyway and the butcher had birds of the king in his possession, and what deal was he talking about anyway? As the butcher didn't have any witnessess to this deal and my uncle knew nothing about it there was an end to it there and then.

Quite a lot of bad deals are settled in this amicable fashion out of court. There was one of the Strangwards of Cambridge once—he is dead now—and he was cheated by a scrap-merchant. There was only perhaps a couple of pounds in the whole deal but the old mush was going to get it off that scrap-merchant if it was the last thing he did. Well, one day he passed the scrap-merchant's and he saw half of a Victorian overmantle out in the front yard—it was the figure of a jumping animal of some kind or other. So he picked it up and walked into the shop and put it on the scale. 'Ah good!', said the scrap-merchant, 'that'll make a pair!', and he paid him quite a good price for it.

There was another story that might be worth telling here and this concerns Manfri Wood, the fisherman on the lake in Bala, Merioneth. Manfri was a very religious man; he was never a poacher at all; he was in fact a gamekeeper and he had a fishing license—but the local water baillie thought that it was unlikely that any Gypsy—even a settled one—would never poach at all. So he was always on the look out, determined to catch

Manfri out. One day Manfri was out with a rod—but he wasn't sitting on the bank, and he wasn't on the boat with Mrs Norie—the *Chiepahnie* (or seagull), as the boat was called—he was out with waders on this occasion, and he wore a long trenchcoat that touched the surface of the water. Through the corner of his eye he could see the water baillie watching him. Well, he kept getting a lot of undersized fish on his hook. Each time he caught one he took it off the hook and put it into the right pocket of his coat—only there was no pocket there at all, just a slit. So the fish dropped back into the water under his coat and swam away. But the water baillie had no idea that this was happening. He waited until he thought that Manfri had about a dozen under-sized fish in his pocket and then he hollered for him to come over to where he was standing. When Manfri got over to him he ordered him to empty his pockets but Manfri refused to do anything of the sort—so it was up to the police station where the water baillie looked pretty ridiculous, and this is how Manfri finally got him off his back.

For the most part there is very little of this sort of lighthearted buffoonery going on in any old-fashioned Romany's life. It was mainly hard work, worry and no play for the great majority of us before the war—though there was a good deal less harassment then than immediately after the war. I had to work very, very hard long before ever I went to school. Almost as soon as I could walk I had to do as much work as a school leaver would do nowadays on his first job—to earn my keep. If we were farming and we had so many acres of land—to hoe the onions, to cut the lettuce, or if we were picking strawberries or raspberries—after the day's work was done, I wasn't finished. I had to help clean the harness, sit round the fire and make pegs, or whip up baskets, or we might have an order for several dozen nets. I'd have to help make these nets. Or if my father had bought some young unbroken ponies—I would have to help break these ponies in; or help clean their coats. There was always something for me to do. I did not have much leisure time at all.

I could not ask my father anything; I could not question anything he did or said and nobody could argue with him. What he said went straight away on the dot or you knew all about it. He was very accurate with his whip and he'd be very quick to use it too. So the older I got the harder I worked. There was always water to fetch; there was always firewood to collect; and when I was a teenager I didn't know what it was to go to a dance, and I hardly knew what it was to go to the pictures. There was always plenty of work for me to do.

Then, when I first went to work in a joinery works— that was Merton Abbey Joinery Works, at a place called Palmers —when I first went to work there and we were staying in the yard, on Saturday afternoons, when all the other young fellows were out, perhaps with their girlfriends, perhaps to go to the pictures or to a dance—not me!—I had work to do; I had to work on trolleys; or on wheels; and of a night-time by the light of an oil lamp my job was to saw up logs with a cross-cut saw. And I did this for many years—I have done this right up till I was army age and I did it again after I came out of the army for several years—right up to the time when I first got married.

I suppose it would have seemed strange to any out-sider who saw all the hard and dirty work we did and then saw us sit down and eat at the table or round the fire in the open. At the table, dinnertime and for other meals, my father was always properly dressed in his best garments with every button done up and not a thread out of place; he was perfectly clean and spotless, with well-manicured fingernails—even though he was a man of the open air—and his diklo, that's his neckscarf, was fastened very tightly at all times; there was never a hair out of place on his head, and dandruff was something he only knew about from hearsay because his hair was regularly shampooed. He insisted that everybody in the family was turned out as well, and as clean, as he was himself—no matter what dirty, messy job they were doing before and after the meal.

My father was always an old man to me; he was an older man to me than either my grandfather or any of my uncles; he had a more old-fashioned outlook on life than anybody else I've ever met. I don't know when he was born but he was in his late middle age when I first noticed him soon after I was a toddler and had to take notice of him rather than my mother;

and he seemed to stay in his late middle age right up to the time I left him. I did not like him very much; he was a very, very hard man, but like everybody else who knew him I did admire, respect and fear him.

Now when we were on the road travelling from place to place, or when we were in the yard, if something came up that had to be discussed, my grandmother was always looked on as the chieftain of the tribe. She was the elder of the tribe and she was always looked on as being the final person to make a decision on whatever subject was under discussion. There was nobody at all over a certain age who was barred from speaking up at these meetings, and she would listen to what everybody had to say and weigh it all up—to get at the feeling of the gathering on the subject, and then at the end she would tell us what the feeling of the meeting was—and that was as good as law. But whatever my father said usually went, because he was in many ways the most practical man in the tribe and his opinions were generally respected. He did not lay down the law—sometimes my grandmother decided against him and he had to accept her decision—but nearly always the rest of the tribe ended up by agreeing with his point of view. When we were travelling the road and something happened in the encampment, they would hold council and the elders of the tribe—my father and my uncles, my grandfather and my grandmother—would sit round the fire and they would have a discussion on what was happening and what they were going to do about it.

Now when we worked on a farm—my aunts, my cousins—boys and girls—my mother, brother and sisters—all the money that was earned was held by my grandmother. She was the banker. The money was collected at different times from the farmer. It was always collected by my father and it was always paid straight to my grandmother; and on a Sunday morning round the fire when the women were present, they would discuss what they were going to do—they would all have so much money out of what had been collected off the farmer—so much to one woman, so much to the other woman, and so much each to the men—and what was left over, which was considerably more than the rest put together, was always looked after by my grandmother—she was the banker, so the tribe would always have money and never go broke; she looked after the common purse of the tribe which was amassed out of the earnings of the women and children of the tribe—the men contributed very little to it. So when I was very young I never knew what it was to have a few shillings given to me to put in my pocket; my money was always looked after by my grandmother or my mother. I never knew what it was to have any money until I was a man old enough to go to work and earn my own money—and the money I had then was very, very little.

When I grew into a man and I decided that I wanted a horse and trolley of my own, and I wanted a wagon of my own, I didn't have any money and I had to go and see my grandmother on a Sunday morning in her wagon to ask her for a grant to buy these things. She asked me if my father had seen the horse, the wagon and the trolley, and if he was satisfied with them, and when I said that he had and that he was satisfied, she lent me the money to make the purchase. To get any kind of loan from my grandmother you had to catch her in the right mood. But whoever borrowed money from the tribe's common purse had to pay back every penny of it—and they were very strict on this—no matter how much of it you had earned for them in the first place in the years of work you had done for them; they thought that if they were good enough to lend you that money to help you out you were obliged to them and indebted to them until you paid it back. If you made no attempt to pay them back what you had borrowed from the common purse—that was the finish of you in the tribe. They would cast you out and never have you back in the tribe any more. This sounds pretty harsh but it was the only way you could be sure that a tribe would survive and that there would always be some ready cash in an emergency.

Now in my family the men were always the head of the family. The men, as the saying goes, always wore the trousers; and what the men said was law. But my mother and my aunts were people who were always respected by their husbands, and they were always given the right to voice their opinions—and as often as not, the women had their way just as long as they didn't try to interfere with their men's business. They knew exactly the position they held; they knew they were there to be housewives, door-to-door sales people, preparers of herbal medicines, nurses in sickness and the mothers of their children; some would be dukkering, that's fortune-telling; some also made lace and embroidery, and they were all pretty good needlewomen and cooks; and all these things were their preserve. They could never tell their men what to do as they did not do the same kinds of things that the men did. There were men's jobs and there were women's jobs and they were kept separate except in serious emergencies when we would all know enough of each other's jobs to be able to co-operate. But the women would never poke their noses into the men's affairs and the men would never poke their noses into the women's affairs.

They were people that were very strict in their morals in every way. We never in my family at all had a divorce anywhere; we never had a woman running away with some-body else's husband, or a man running off with somebody else's wife. We never had a girl have an illegitimate child—because in my family this was something that would never have been for-given. If, with her own consent, the girl had got herself into trouble and had a child, she would have been banished from the tribe; they would never have anything to do with her again—they would have taken this as a disgrace.

Once a couple were married in our tribe the wife had to keep her place and always be a credit to her husband. She always had to be dressed respectably when she walked out, with her dress down to her ankles. A woman in my family, if she was going out in the morning, and somebody spoke to her, or just said 'Good morning', she would never answer—they would only greet people they knew well. Their code was very, very strong; and myself as a teenager, and my cousins, boys and girls, we were looked to keep up that moral code—if a strange woman spoke to any of us lads, we were not supposed to answer either. If I walked into a shop unattended by one of my parents or an uncle and there was a woman serving in the shop, I walked out again. This was also the case with my cousins—we never contacted any women—any strange woman in any way at all unless we were in the company of some of the older members of the tribe. If we travelled by public transport, which wasn't very often, if there was a vacant seat and it meant sitting beside a woman, we'd sooner stand up than sit down. This was a code that was carried right through my family. And when the women went out calling and they knocked at a door and a woman came out, they would start offering her what was in their baskets, but if a man answered the door, they would ask for the lady of the house, and if there was no lady there, they would walk away without doing any business. And the girls were never allowed to wear make-up; they were never allowed to leave a button undone; and they were never allowed to take their shoes off in front of anybody; they were very, very strict in these things in every way—too strict!

In lots of Romany families the wives are chosen for the sons; and in my case, from the time I was very small, a girl was chosen for me to marry; and as I grew older, at times this was brought up—especially round the camp-fire. They would ramble on and on about what was going to happen when we got married, and how well suited we were for one another—but, of course, I couldn't stand that girl they had chosen for me, and she couldn't stand me, and anyway I knew I was going to marry Anna right from the time we were small children together— and she detested the boy they'd chosen for her too. So the tribe's plans didn't come off in our case at all because I chose this girl, who is my wife and the mother of my two children, for myself already when I was very, very young. What's more, she also knew whom she was going to marry, come what may. We went and collected firewood together; we went and fetched water together; we paddled in the stream together when we went fishing a few odd times; we've also been poaching together with the grown-ups, and when I finally grew into a teenager and I went to work in the joinery works, my wife left home and went into service. She went to work into hospitals—she moved into one hospital, working and living in, stayed there for some years and then moved to another hospital. But we always kept in close contact. Whenever I could I always slipped off to see her, and then one day I decided that it was about time I got married, I went to see her and asked her, wasn't it about time that we jumped the broomstick—which is a saying when two Romany people first go off together, even if they don't jump any broomstick at all. She knew exactly what I had at the time, which wasn't very much, as any reader can work out from what I wrote on the common purse, but I did have a horse, a wagon and a set of harness of my own; and I had a pony and trolley as well as some very smart clothes—and this was important as my wife-to-be was a very smart woman indeed. I told her that we would get married in the normal way in a church if that was what she wanted but that I would prefer to do it in the Romany way. When I spoke to my parents about marrying her they were very resentful as they had chosen somebody else for me—so I had no more to say about it and kept this thing to myself from then on. I decided on a date to go off. I spent all my spare cash on sheets and blankets, crockery, cutlery and extra pots and pans and so forth, and I rigged my wagon out as it should be for a young couple. I painted it all up and at the time we'd chosen, a Saturday, I put my horse and wagon, pony and trolley and all the rest of my belongings into one of my uncle's yards where I was welcome, and then drove my horse and wagon straight over to a pre-arranged point where I met my bride. We went off a-travelling on our own for several weeks before we went back to my uncle's place to fetch my pony and trolley. From then on and for about another two years I drove the horse and wagon and my wife drove the pony and trolley. We travelled all over Kent, Surrey and Essex for nearly two years before we decided to have children. When we decided to have children we thought it was about time we got properly married.

I went to see a parson and explained the position to him. He told me he could marry us in the normal way—which would have meant putting up the banns—or he could marry us on a special licence. I did not care for the first possibility as my people might have heard of the banns being put up, and my wife's people might have heard about it, and they would definitely have come along to cause trouble at the wedding. So I decided to get married on a special licence. They made all the arrangements, the special licence was put in for, went through and arrived back on the following Friday. Next day we got married at three hours' notice. The two witnesses were people we had never seen before —they were passers-by off the road, a milkman and a sweep— and we worked it this way to avoid our families causing trouble at the wedding. To get married cost me £3 8s. 9d. It was all very solemn.

We went back to the wagon and discussed what sort of family we were going to have. We decided to have a son for a start and a daughter after. But somehow we bungled it; it didn't work out that way. We had a daughter and a son all right but we had the daughter first and the son afterwards. My wife's name is Anna, my daughter is called Sally and my son is Robin. Now, as I am telling the story, my daughter is a girl of fourteen and I think she will end up standing at around six foot or more; she's got hair right back to the bends of her knees but unlike the old Romany girls she wears the same clothes as any other girl of this day and age. Robin, my son, is a very nice lad indeed—he is very, very clever in poaching, the same as I am—a very good son; and he is very clever in many other ways too; my children are very good with the ferrets and with anything to do with outdoors, and they can paint and draw very good pictures and they are not bad at school. We were never going to have more than two children as two is the most that a couple on its own can bring up properly.

Now, after my wife and I travelled together for some time, I did meet up with the family again at different times but it was none too pleasant, so we decided to go by different routes from the rest to avoid them and we have therefore always been on our own since then. This has thrown us on our own resources and cut us off from the common purse. So we have on occasion been in tight straits—but by and large we were probably better off and certainly more relaxed than in the old days.

I want to go back in my story now to the time when I was a teenager. I want to go back to the time when we were travelling as a tribe. My grandfather was a man who was always very clever with woodwork and other things, as I told you before, but he was also a man that always kept one of the old Romany traditional trades a-going, and that was the keeping of trotting horses. He always had a trotter; and my father always had a trotter. Well, my grandfather had a horse and he had the blood of these horses for many years; and his father, old Thomas Wood, in Wales, had the blood of this horse before him. The blood of this horse they kept, colt or filly, and they bred different blood into that strain to keep it in a certain line; and at the time I am talking about now, on Mitcham Common, from the Red House to the Blue House, which was a straight mile—horses were always run across this way and paced across there; my grandfather, and also my father, won a lot of money across Mitcham Common with racing his horses against other people's trotters, especially of a holiday time. Now, my grandfather had this filly which was a pedigree horse, and he decided that the time had come, and this was the right type of horse, to put to a racehorse.

So he went a-mushgaying—which is another way of saying, he went a-spying out the land—and so did my uncles at Epsom, all around the stud-farms and they selected the horse he was going to use, but naturally the owner would never have agreed to let him use his stallion to mate with his filly, and so they could only mate them when it was out on grass—which was a difficult proposition as you could only get at it through the fields and had to avoid getting anywhere near the stables; also you had to know when the racehorse was out on grass and not in the stable—and so the thing was not nearly as simple as it may appear to be. When everything had been spied out we went to Epsom with this filly and put the mare to this racehorse in the field late at night. Coming from Epsom Downs at half past three in the morning my grandfather was stopped by a policeman. He told the policeman some fantastic story and the policeman let him go.

Well, he looked after this mare like you would look after a woman in childbirth and when she had this foal he called it Fireworks. When this Fireworks was adult it was broken in to pull a trotting gig—it was a light bay in colour and exceptionally fast in every way. In the front it was all trotter but behind it was all racehorse. When we took it to pace it across Mitcham Common, there is a road halfway across Mitcham Common called Windmill Road, and that was going to be the road where we were going to set this horse really full a-going; and we started at the Red House and waited till the road was clear. I had my father's black mare, my grandfather had his Fireworks and we started level and we started off; and when we got to Windmill Road my grandfather said to the horse, 'Go on Fireworks, set them alight!', and although I tried everything I could to catch her, I could not. She was at the Blue House and finished while I was still trying to get up speed, well behind on the road. This Fireworks was a very fast horse in every way—over a long or a short distance—and my grandfather was bid quite a lot of money for her. At different places in the country where he'd raced other people, they would never race him again because she was far too fast.

Now I want to go still further back in my story to the time when I was a youngster, and at this particular time we were stopping in the yard during the summer months over some business or other. It was a very hot summer; the yard was at Merton and near by was a meadow called Bunces Meadow. This meadow belonged to Lord George Hatfield who also owned a big park which was called Hatfield Park. The meadow was at the back of the park at the other side of the railway; and through this meadow the river Wandle ran. In those days the river was very, very clean, and being as the weather was very, very hot we were down in the meadow a-bathing in the river, a-swimming. In a place near by, in an old patch that they used to call the Dust, there were some Pikies stopping there on this Dust. Now, one of these Pikie boys had a lurcher dog and he also had a little Black Forest pony. He was sitting on this pony's back and came riding up the meadow. When he reached to where we were, he jumped off the pony's back and into the river with all his clothes on. We asked him why he wouldn't take his clothes off but he wouldn't tell us, so we ducked him under the water. When we got out of the water he got out too—we were wrestling on the grass—one of the other lads who was with us looked up and said, 'Oh, look at that pony! she's got a wart on her tummy'— and sure enough on the pony's tummy there was a wart as big as a bread and butter plate. I said to this Pikie lad, 'That poor blooming horse—why are you riding it with such a wart on its tummy?', and he told me that his father had taken it to different places to try and get it done, but nobody would do the operation. The

cause of this wart was that the horse had had a harness on that was too big, and with the movement of the trolley that it was pulling on the road, the horse's seesawing caused a friction on its tummy that gradually developed into a growing wart. The lad told me his father had taken it to the Blue Cross Hospital at New Cross, and they refused to touch it.

Now, when we were lads we were always the same as the men when we were amongst horses and ponies. We always opened the horse's or pony's mouth to see what age it was, and we discussed the various good and bad points in a horse amongst ourselves the same as the men would. Now, by the teeth of this black forest pony I could tell that it was only a youngster. It seemed a shame that a horse so young should have to be put down. The lad had told us that his father was going to sell it to the knacker-man, which is what we would have called a horse slaughter man.

When we got home that evening we told my uncle Jerry about this poor pony, and my father, who was some distance away, understood that we were talking about a pony and he came up to us to find out what was wrong. So we told him. My father would not normally have anything to do with Didikais or Pikies—he would deal only with Romanies and the gentry and the odd Gorgios as a rule—but when I told him how old I thought this pony was he decided to make an exception in this case, even though it meant dealing with some of the worst type of Pikies, and he would go there and operate to save the pony's life. He sent me there and then over to the man it belonged to, to tell him that we would be over to where he was encamped at ten o'clock the following Sunday morning to perform the operation.

That Sunday, while this operation was going on, I looked under one of the wagons that these Pikies had and there was a dog there tied up with a little bit of short rope to the back axle—there was hardly enough rope to let the dog lie down. She was a long-haired lurcher bitch that had had pups on her, and she was as poor as a crow—you could see every one of her ribs; her coat was matted with burrs; and she was also covered in clay and mud. I said to the bloke she belonged to—

the mush, as we'd call him, whom it belonged to—'For Christ's sake, don't let my father see that or else he'll set about you with a whip!' The man in the wagon said to me, 'You can have the dog if you want it', and I turned round to the man and said, 'If this dog was any good you would not give it to me'. He said, 'Well, the reason I'm going to give you this dog is it's a marked dog and if I let it go the gamekeeper or somebody else round here is bound to shoot it, and that's why I'm keeping it tied up.' So out of pity's sake I undid the dog from the piece of rope and led it up to my father's yard without him seeing it.

My father came straight back from the operation, and when he saw the dog tied up in the yard he nearly went berserk, because we had quite a lot of whippets and whippet-lurchers and bush-dogs up the yard at the time and he did not want another dog there unless it was perfectly clean and healthy. He could see that this dog was covered in vermin. He was going to shoot it—but I was only young and I started crying so he relented just this once. This was the only day I can remember my father doing things against his better judgment—first the pikie's pony, then the dog. He told me to fill the copper up with water in the yard and start the fire going underneath. I filled the copper up with water from the pump and lit a woodfire in the brick-work oven underneath. Then my father sent me out to get a gallon of paraffin. When I got back from the shop the water was already boiling. As soon as I handed him the paraffin, my father poured it all over the dog. He said that was to kill the fleas, ticks and other vermin and that you've got to be cruel to be kind. The dog nearly went mad when my father poured the paraffin over him. After letting the dog soak in paraffin for some time, we filled up a tin bath and bathed the dog in warm water and carbolic soap. Then my father clipped all the burrs out of its coat and pulled all the tangles out with a horse comb. He then put it back in the bath and bathed it again—to make sure. It was then put in an empty stable with some straw and a good feed of biscuits. The dog scoffed up the biscuits and my father told me not to give it anything else to eat as this could do it more harm than good. He said, 'We'll give it a little and often', and after a few days of this, it was a different dog entirely.

After we had this dog several weeks my father told me that if she did not work I would have to get rid of her—he thought she was quite a useless dog—but my uncle said no, we shouldn't—she was a good dog and he could always tell a good dog when he saw one—so we waited until September came round, and my father said, 'Now we'll find out if the dog can work—and if she won't, we'll get rid of her.'

On the Sunday morning we were all going out ferreting—my father, uncle Jerry and all the youngsters. We had several other dogs with us. Well, we worked on one particular farm where we had permission to catch the rabbits, and my bitch did not show much intelligence where rabbits were concerned at all; she never seemed to be too keen to work a bush—in fact she did nothing at all. We bolted a few rabbits with a ferret and the other dogs turned one or two rabbits out of the bushes.

We shifted from that farm to a poultry farm where we poached for rabbits in a field behind some trees and shrubbery. We hadn't been there for very long when this bitch came up with a chicken in her mouth; she dropped the chicken on the ground, she hadn't put a feather out of place or harmed the chicken in any way, and she went off and in no time at all she was back with another chicken; and before we could do anything about it she was back with a third chicken. So my father told me to put the lead on her; and my uncle said, 'You see what I mean, now, I always said she is a good dog, and she is a good dog—she is a kanniechor—didn't I tell you I could always tell a good dog?'

I put the lead on her. My uncle asked me if I would let him have this dog as he had been looking for one like it for a long time and in the finish, after a few weeks of having to keep him tied up in the yard I gave this dog to my uncle. Normally this would not have been the kind of dog a Romany would keep—it was a pikie dog, and anyone but my uncle would have been drummed out of the tribe for keeping it, and using it too, for wherever we travelled and whatever part of the country we were in, we always had chicken for dinner as long as this bitch was alive. We realized that this must have been the reason that this was a marked dog and that this was the reason I was given it in the first place. It was a wanted dog, a kanniechor—a chicken thief—and by Christ, she could chor a kannie! She earned my uncle many pounds at this game as she would pick a chicken up without hurting it—she wouldn't damage it in any way and she would carry it to you and drop it at your feet. We often tried to train another dog as good as this one for picking up game fowl in the same way, or wild ducks and geese, though not chickens; we even tried to train some of the pups, but we never ever did have one as good as this dog—we had exceptionally good dogs to take a bird but never another one to come up to this one. She could take any bird, whether it was on dry land or on the water; if it was a goose or a duck she was just the same—and I've known the time when she has even tackled a big stag turkey. I've seen her dragging this turkey along by his neck. And we kept her right until the day she died, this bitch.

3   The Old Wardos

Every tribe had something that made it stand out. In Wales our tribe was famous for its pure speech; in the Roberts branch, for its great harpers, some of whom became harpers to Queen Victoria in the 1870s. I remember my father showing me an engraving with all the harpers of the Roberts family—who were cousins of his—playing before Queen Victoria. That engraving was used in a magazine at the time to illustrate the story of the harpers of Wales.

Matthew Wood and his sons were well-known naturalists around Bala, great fisherman, fiddlers, step-dancers and, some of them, very popular story-tellers. They were greatly respected in the area and they were pillars of the church for generations.

Our own branch of the tribe, and the Ingrams also, were best known for horse-breeding and doctoring, wood-carving and wagon-building.

I have travelled all over the British Isles, doing seasonal farmwork, horse-dealing, carpentry and joinery—all the other Gypsy work I will describe in the next chapter—and building wagons.

We never travelled in the winter months; this was the time for shoeing horses, repairing and repainting wagons and other maintenance work. This was also the time to start on any new wagons that had to be built, either for a customer or as a replacement for one of our own. As far as I know, we and the Ingrams were the only two tribes in England who actually built wagons from scratch. If we had to build a wagon we used to start work on it as soon as we got into our winter quarters in the yard.

The very first part of a wagon you build is the wheels. A wagon wheel has several parts. They are called 'the felleys', 'the spokes', 'the stock' or 'hub', and 'the tyre'. The felleys is the part of a wheel that is on the outside under the iron rib or tyre. We always kept a good store of seasoned oak and ash hidden in the yard for making the felleys which we marked out and cut from one of the templates that we kept hanging in the stable. All the lads of the tribe in those days had to take a hand at cutting the felleys. They were cut by hand to form a wheel-section, on part of a circle, and the ends of each section or felley were bored to take a dowel, which is a pin of wood or iron inserted to fasten the felleys together—with us it was always hardwood dowels of the measurement three inches by one inch. All the sockets or bores had to be drilled very accurately into the felleys. As to the size, there were different templates for the various sizes of wheels we made in the yard.

The next things were the spokes, made of larch, if possible, or of ash. The spokes were first split down roughly from pieces of wood that were cut to a certain length; they were then roughly drawn into shape with a drawknife—and all the boys and young lads had to take their turn in doing these, being watched over by one of my uncles or my grandfather. When all the spokes for a particular wheel were drawn into shape, one end of each spoke was cut to a chisel point and the other to form a dowel. This dowel went into a felley and the other end went into the stock. Here again it was essential that the bores and slits in the felleys and the stock were accurately placed and put in at the correct angles. When all the spokes were ready they were laid aside until we had done the stock.

The stock is the round hollow piece of wood, usually made of oak or elm, that goes in the centre, which is called the hub. After this had been turned down on a lathe, which we used to work on a treadle, it was placed in a hole in the concrete yard, where we had moulds to take several sizes of wheels—and the stock was always the first thing we placed in the hole in the centre; then the spokes were entered into the stock and the felleys were fitted onto the spokes. When all this was complete, the next thing was to put on the tyre.

The tyre was put on red hot—it was made of iron. Buckets of water were placed round the wheel; later we changed to using a hose-pipe. When the tyre was ready it was lifted onto the wheel with tongs. This was in a way the trickiest part of the operation as you had to be very quick and accurate at the same time and the iron had to be as hot as possible before you cooled it down very quickly with the water. As the tyre was knocked onto the wheel with a hammer, the water was thrown onto the wheel. This made the tyre shrink and tighten the wheel up. It also hardened the metal.

The wheel was now ready to take the box. The box is the bearing that goes in the hollow of the stock in the centre of the wheel. It is made of gun metal or iron, and it is tapered with two flanges—a flange being a projecting or raised edge or flank on a wheel—at either end. The box is got ready with a piece of sacking wound round, and when it is driven into the stock with a boxwood mallet, the sack enables the box to move. It is then placed on the spindle and spun round to see if the wheel runs true. If it does not run true, the sacking will enable you to move the wheel in whatever direction necessary until it does run true. You then drive wedges in between the stock and the box to hold it firm. Then you pour on a resin glue which bonds it permanently onto the spindle The basis of this glue is the same as what is used for bird-lime but with an additional ingredient and in a much thicker consistency.

Now, to go through the materials you would use for making a wagon-wheel, and some of the tricks of the trade of a Romany wheelwright. The tyre you got as stock from a metal merchant; you could not generally get it in the country but had to go to London or some other big city for it. The rest of the materials were all local stuff or things we produced ourselves. For instance, there was the business of wedding the stock and the box to the shaft. The hole in the centre is tapered, and what we used to do was to knock in the shaft with a mallet—with a piece of sacking round the shaft—so that there was a certain amount of play. You'd drive the shaft in until it was level with the face of the stock. So you have now got that wheel on a spindle and you spin it round to see if it is buckled. If it is buckled, the sacking that you had rolled round the end of the shaft would give you the amount of movement you want to push it one way or the other to get that wheel to run true. Well, when we got that wheel to run true we used to pack it out with hard wooden wedges—those wedges were either of seasoned beech or oak. You knock the first load of wedges in lightly, and then we used to knock wedges at the side of them a bit tighter, and we used to wedge right the way round until they were all tight and well inside the box or bearing. The glue we used on those wedges, to bond them in, was made out of the bark of a holly tree—we got the bark of a holly tree and boiled it right down with another ingredient in water, and the glue used to run just like treacle when it was hot. Without the second ingredient that was disolved in the water we would have got bird-lime, but this way you got something very hard once it was set. You had to melt it each time you wanted to use it just like ordinary pearl glue.

Shafts were sometimes made out of well-seasoned ash; stocks could be made of oak, felleys of ash, and spokes of ash—but I think it is best if you make the stock of oak or beech or any other kind of hardwood if you cannot get hold of these, and you make the spokes of larch—with larch you have got a certain amount of spring, and if you make the felleys of good seasoned oak or good seasoned ash and you do happen to be in rough country, or happen to run up a curve, it is nearly always the ends of the spokes that break on a wheel. If the spokes are made of larch you've got a certain amount of spring, so instead of them snapping off, they'll move to a certain extent and then spring back into position—so nine times out of ten you won't get a broken spoke. You see, once larch is seasoned, it is as hard as iron—it is a soft wood when you first fell it, but it is very hard when it is seasoned. Woods like willow or pine will crack under very low stress—that is why pinestubbs are used down mines; they will start to crack with quite loud snapping sounds some minutes before they actually break. This is a sign that the load they bear has somehow shifted—perhaps due to a landslide overhead—and that it is essential to clear out as quickly as possible. Any other wood might snap right away without any warning and bury the miners alive.—But on a wagon-wheel it is best to use something that does not break too easily and in my experience larch is the best material for spokes.

When the four wheels are complete you start on the undercarriage. The biggest job on that is the lock. This is the turntable on the front. The wood used for this was normally straight-grained ash. The mortice and tenon had to be cut out and picked out and the lock put together and fitted onto an iron circle. This circle enabled the lock to turn easily.

Then you started on the main chassis of the wagon. The runners and cross-members, which are the equivalent of the joists and floorboards in a house, were selected and were morticed and tenoned, put together, wedged and glued. Then you came to the axle-bearers which were big pieces of timber that used to sit on top of the axle. These were ornamentally carved with several designs (mainly to reduce their weight with-out reducing their strength) and after they were carved they were picked out in all different colours.

When the undercarriage was completed the springs were attached to it with bolts, and the undercarriage was attached to the lock. Then you put on the shafts—which were nearly always bought already made, though sometimes we made our own—and fitted on the wheels in the way I have already described.

Then the 'kettle-box' for carrying the pots and pans was fitted out at the back of the wagon, in between the wheels. This was wedded to the pull-bar-horse.

All the other timber for finishing the wagon was got ready and packed onto this undercarriage on wheels, as it took several weeks to accomplish this part of the job because most of the time we would be earning our living doing other things. The women used to go 'calling'—hawking with the baskets; the men had markets to attend with horses; also we had to go out with logs and other things to earn our living. The wagon was done mostly in our spare time and when the weather was too bad to do anything else. The stove and the heavy equip-ment to go into the wagon was always carried on another wagon when we started travelling in February or March. The skeleton of the wagon was pulled by a spare horse that was here specially for the purpose.

When we got to our first stopping place, every night, after we had finished our farmwork, each member of the tribe would do a little bit to the wagon. The uprights, or walls, would be got ready, and the tenons cut; the mortices would be cut into sole pieces and the tenons entered into the mortices—and these used to be set in with the resin glue of the holly tree that I have described already. We would do a little bit of this each night until it got dark and we would also work on it weekends; and as we travelled from place to place doing farmwork and other work, each place we went to, the wagon grew. So by the time we finished our round of the travelling that season, when we got back to the yard we had a finished article—we had a wagon that was finished, made by hand and painted and varnished by hand; and some of our wagons can still be seen on the roads of England today.

4 Work and Play

I have never met a Gypsy or a traveller who has a hobby. Life is a hobby in itself; live it to the full and try and take an intelligent interest in every job you do, and there is no need for you to just kill time. A Gorgio will go out for a walk or a drive merely for the sake of walking or driving—but a Gypsy won't; he must have some reason for doing so; he is studying the lay of the land, or the movements of the gamekeeper, or the habits of the game in the locality—in case he hits a bad spell and is obliged to go after food; or he is advertising the fact that he is in the area, where he is known and had a reputation for doing this, that, or the other job, as well or better than any of the locals. Even when he does appear to be at play—for instance singing and dancing, gambling, or doing a chop, it is with a view to something extra in the pocket earned more pleasantly a few miles further on. Everything that is not done for profit right away can be described as a practice run for next week's struggle. Even quite a fearful row in which the various members of a tribe knock each other black and blue is more often than not started quite deliberately by two or more of the head people to keep everybody in good fighting trim, just in case there is some serious trouble ahead. So a Gypsy has all the excitement he needs, all the fun and pleasure that a Gorgio has to dream up for himself artificially, but it comes to him as a bonus in the course of his everyday life.

The work of a Gypsy in the old way could be put under several headings. There was farmwork; there was hunting, poaching and pest control; there was basket-making, peg-making, net-making, lace-making, artificial-flower-making, wood-carving and metalwork, patching and mending; there was

45

horse-breeding, dog-breeding and ferret-breeding; there was forestry work; timber-yard work; grinding of knives, shears, scythes, sickles, axes and so forth; there was also dry-saltery —which is making up of natural dyes and colours and chalks; there was hedging, ditching and wattle-hurdling fences and gates. Markets had to be attended and the woman had to go on their calls.

Farmwork has changed considerably over the past few years; in some areas it has almost completely dried up as a means of earning a living for the Gypsies. Many of the seasonal jobs are now done in a seemingly more efficient way, mechanically—probably too wasteful and unnatural in their waste of natural manures, straw, soil-conserving organisms and living things such as useful insects and worms that tended to preserve the fertility of the soil in the past. As the soil becomes more and more arid it will become increasingly more obvious that a return to good husbandry is essential if we are not to turn the whole country into a desert. It is only to be hoped that the farmers and the people they will employ will remember the various techniques of good husbandry when the present fun and games have finally to stop.

My father and two of my uncles were the only Romanies I know of who were sometimes hired as ploughmen. Apart from that most of our farmwork had to do with harvesting and storing. One of the things we used to do that I have not seen done for many years in the Home Counties was making potato clamps. A potato clamp is a long, deep, oblong pit lined with straw. When the straw is laid out in the pit the potatoes are stacked on it and built up above the top of the pit to form the shape of the roof of a house; this roof-shape is covered with straw and the straw is covered all over with earth—tufts of straw stick out through the earth for ventilation. The potatoes— and other root crops too—were stored in such clamps until they were sold.

Often as not, my father hired out two or three of his horses for carting the root crops to the clamps. When we pulled swedes we chopped the tops off with a knife or a billhook before we clamped them. These crops were paid by the hundredweight. Onions were paid by the acre, but grain—wheat, barley and so forth—was paid at so much an hour.

When harvesting wheat and other grain the work-gangs were split up into specialist work-groups. At the head of the gang were the cutters or mowers who worked either with horse-drawn mowers, or, if the ground was unsuitable for this, with scythes or sickles. Behind them came the binders—usually women—who gathered up and bound the mown stalks into sheaves; and behind them came the stookers. Their job was to stook the sheaves. A stook is eight sheaves—four to a side—stood head to head against each other to air and dry out the grain in the wind before it can germinate. A stooker takes a sheaf under each arm, pushes the heads of the two sheaves against each other to entwine the ears of the grain and firmly pushes the bottoms down on the earth so that the two sheaves stand quite solidly on the ground; the next two sheaves are made to lean slightly against these first two, and the other two pairs of sheaves in the stook are placed to lean against the first two pairs from the opposite side in the stook. There generally was one cutter or mower to one stooker to three or four binders, but later on, when the cutter-binders came in, there was just one man working the mechanical horse-drawn cutter that cut and bound at the same time, to a gang of ten to fifteen stookers. There were farms before the war where the whole job was done by Romanies and travellers.

When the stooks were dried, the leading-in job came next. The stooks were loaded onto a special horse-drawn cart with two-pronged hay forks. One man on top stacked them. He had to be very careful not to get the prongs stuck into the palms of his hands. The carts took the unthreshed grain to a prepared site where it was built up into ricks ready for the miller to take away. I still remember some farms before the war where the grain was taken straight into a barn and threshed straight away with flails, stored in a special loft for some time, where it was turned frequently until it was dry enough to be put into sacks for the miller to cart away—but, as far as I am aware none of this is done in this way at the present time—but I am convinced that in another century some such methods will have

47

to be reintroduced, particularly the use of the horse, of straw and other natural products, as well as natural manures and means of pest control.

In the past pest control was one of my tribe's specialities. A pest is an insect, a bird, a virus or an animal or weed whose natural enemy has become extinct. In the past the natural enemy of the rabbit and the woodpigeon was the fox. The fox was overhunted because it also attacked poultry and other domestic animals such as sheep, and so rabbits and woodpigeons became a pest. Clearly it would have been cheaper and better to improve the fences around poultry farms, duck ponds and grazing land to keep out foxes, rather than hunt them down and create a plague of rabbits and woodpigeons that cause far more damage than the fox ever did—but until the rabbit and pigeon plagues afflicted us such an idea never occurred to anyone, and even today there are quite a lot of people who think that foxes should be exterminated. Three other animals that should never have been hunted were the weasel, the stoat and the polecat. They also kept down rabbits, pigeons, and all kinds of rodents—particularly rats. They were rather more useful in keeping a good balance of wild life than was the fox, as they rarely attacked domestic animals at all. Yet for many years all-out war was waged against weasels, stoats and polecats—except for a small number that were inter-bred into ferrets for rat-catching and rabbitting. Just as foxes, weasels and stoats were important for keeping down certain classes of small animals, so certain insects were important for keeping down other insects. For instance the ladybird eats all sorts of grubs that are harmful to crops and young seedling trees; and so it is with all living things in nature, animals, plants and insects as well as birds, making it possible for each other to exist by giving off nourishment and keeping a right balanced breathable air all the time, while at the same time keeping down each others numbers to a manageable size.

The most profitable pest control commissions came from farmers whose barns and outhouses were overrun by rats. For rat control we used ferrets and dogs. These we bred and trained ourselves. A whole book could be written on ferrets alone; here I will just describe one typical rat control operation.

A farmer had agreed to my price for clearing his farm of rats. I went to his farm and found that there were rat holes under the floors and in the linings of every building there. I told him that I would come back in a few days with some ferrets and nets to catch these rats. Rat nets are made out of silk or nylon stockings and bean tins with the top and bottom cut out. The tin is put in the top of the stocking which is then tightened round the tin with a piece of string. You push the open end of the tin into the rat hole. When the rat comes out it passes through the tin into the stocking. With the tin being there you could, if you had to, pick the rat up without being bitten. I took several such nets to the farm and brought my ferrets in a box and my dogs at my heels.

I first chose a burrow to ferret under a chicken-house floor. I placed two dogs on one side of the building, one dog on the other side, and myself with a bag of pebbles and a catapult in front. I put one of my ferrets under the floor and placed the net in the hole—I pushed the tin that was in the top of the stocking in the hole behind the ferret—and as soon as the ferret was out of sight we could hear the rats making a noise under the floor. By the noise that was made I could tell that one ferret would not be enough, so I took another ferret out of the box and put it down another hole into the burrow in the same way as I had placed the first one. We heard some rustling noises, some thumping noises, and then the rats started to bolt through the tins into the stockings. As they bolted into the stockings I cracked them with pebbles out of my catapult. The few odd rats that bolted out of openings that I had not netted each side of the building the dogs finished off. Within ten minutes all the rats under the chicken-house floor were killed. There were about twenty-five of them.

I took my dogs and ferrets to another part of the farm between an outhouse and a pigeon shed. There was a mound of earth which originally had been a rockery. This was honey-combed with rat holes. I netted up most of the holes and covered the rest with stones. I turned one of my ferrets in and we waited. One rat showed just its nose and one of my dogs pulled it straight out by its nose and killed it. This dog, a Jack Russell, had waited in that place as the stone that I had placed over a hole there had moved, and she killed seventeen rats there in about ten minutes. The ferret that I had put in didn't come out—we waited and waited, but he didn't come out. I realized that he had either killed a female in the hole or got into a nest of youngsters and settled down for a feast. There are two ways of getting a laid-up ferret out of a hole. One is to let off a big banger—the sort you get for Guy Fawkes Day—at one of the holes. For some reason that has never been explained the ferret will come out by this hole just as soon as the smoke begins to clear. Sometimes a second banger will have to be let off before the ferret comes up. If it still does not come up it is probably dead. The other method to retrieve a laid-up ferret is to dig it out. On this occasion I decided to dig.

I placed my dogs into the positions I thought the rats would bolt from as soon as I moved, and then I started to dig with a spade. I also had a dog digging and she told me where the nest was. I came across the remains of two very large rats—one male and one female—which were probably the original pair that started the colony, the parents of all the other rats we had killed as they bolted. I then found a nest of ten baby rats, each of which was bitten clean in half by the ferret; and then I found the ferret a-winking her whiskers and blinking her eyes at me. I picked her up and put her in the box with the other ferrets. That afternoon we got rid of all the rats on the farm. There were over ninety altogether, and that was not a large number as rats go. Dogs and ferrets is the surest, quickest and cheapest way of getting rid of rats that I know of.

The favourite dog with most Romanies is a lurcher. This is a cross-breed between a greyhound or a whippet and a sheepdog—but there are varieties arrived at when this basic kind of lurcher is further crossed with a whippet-foxterrier cross-breed; these two cross-breeds are sometimes interbred with a saluki before being crossed with each other. But quite frequently a pure-bred whippet is preferred, and for bush-dogs some terriers are more suitable than other breeds. I prefer to use Jack Russells for when a small dog is needed and a whippet for everything else, as whippets are more intelligent and good dogs for a short distance. As I have shown, dogs can be trained to work as a team with other dogs and with ferrets. But when you go hunting or coursing a single dog is often sufficient.

If I am after a particular hare I count on having two separate sessions—one on studying its habits and one to get it. The first session you locate your hare, work it up the field to see which way it will run and where it will go for cover. The next session you will come with your dog.

One day in a particular field in Surrey where I had walked up a hare some time before, I took a long stick with me, a catapult, some stones and the dog at my heel. I walked around the field until I was upwind. I left the dog sitting in a corner of the field and circled right round the hare and walked towards it till I got within about thirty yards of it. It could see me and had my scent. Another five yards closer and the hare would have bolted and we would have lost it. I stood perfectly still for a few seconds. Then I pushed the stick into the ground, took off my coat very slowly and hung my hat and coat onto the stick. The idea of this was that the hare should not lose my scent as I edged away from the stick with my coat—and scent—on it. I made my way to the nearest cover behind the stick then walked back to where my dog was upwind from the hare. Meantime the hare kept sitting watching my stick with my hat and coat on. I walked right round the back of the hare with the dog as close as I could get to it—and then I clapped my hands as a signal to my dog, and to set the hare a-running at the same time—and the dog took chase. As I went to put my coat on, the dog ran down the field. The hare made a left turn to run up the field, the dog turned him again and the hare was mine. On this occasion I had no need for a catapult at all. The reason for the strategy I described is that in a straightforward way you can not generally get close enough to a hare to catch it—so you must put it off its guard.

Another important art that brought in a livelihood as well as some food for the pot was net-making. There were many different kinds of nets for which there was always a ready sale in some parts of the country. All these nets we also made for our own use. A lot of these nets were for catching song-birds for hybridizing with canaries. The simplest type to make was called a trap-net or a ditch-net. This was one of very fine mesh about five foot square placed between two nets of the same size but with a mesh four inches square. If, for instance, you were going after bullfinches, you would place the net in a gap in the hedgerow over a ditch which bullfinches were using; both the net and the string that secured it would be very dull in colour and so the bullfinches would not see it. Now you select the bird you wish to catch and walk it up the hedge—it will keep flying and hopping in the direction of the net and eventually fly into it. As the bird hits the net through the big mesh into the small mesh, its flight is broken, but the impact carries it through the other big mesh. The small mesh now forms a pocket which holds the bird securely, as the weight of its belly folds the small mesh at the top. All you have to do now is to pick him up and put him in your stocking box. A stocking box is a carrying cage about nine inches in length and width and about six inches deep. It has three wooden sides and wire mesh in front. On top you have a hole cut with a stocking attached from the inside, leading into it. You take your bird in one hand and put it into the box through the stocking, let it go, withdraw your hand and tie the stocking into a knot. You can carry several birds in one stocking box—and you can take any of them out at will without it, or any of the others having a chance to get away. Bullfinches were used for mule breeding with canaries and then let go.

Another type of trap-net also used for catching a variety of birds was constructed like a giant mousetrap. It is a trap-net on the ground made of wire with a string mesh-net over it. To make it you first bend two identical lengths of wire into a half circle each and lay one on top of the other and then attach strong springs at the ends to hold them together tightly; the mesh-net is now fitted on. Next, one half of the circle is pegged down on the ground. The other half is prised open and held in position with a strong wooden stick that is pegged down at one end, goes over the jaw of the trap-net and somewhere near the middle of the circle is held by a hairsbreadth with a T-shaped piece of wood. When you have set the net you scatter some seeds on the ground outside the circle to form a path, and some more inside the circle and quite a lot around the T-shaped piece. Now you start to walk up your birds—as many as you can manage at one time—and if you know what you are about, eventually one of them will knock over the T-shaped piece. When he does this, the top half of the net will fly over and any birds inside the net will be ready for you to put into your stocking box. There were nearly twenty different ways of catching song-birds, several of them employing nets, call-birds and brace-birds. Here again a whole book could be written on the subject—but perhaps it better had not. Peg-birds, clap-nets, bat-nets and so on would have to be described in detail with diagrams; the making of bird-lime out ot the bark of the holly tree or from mistletoe boiled up with water; water-proofing bird-lime with shoe polish and a lot of other tricks of the trade could be described in great detail—but this is an old trade that had perhaps best be discontinued rather than encouraged.

The greater number of nets we used to make for sale. Most of these were not for song-birds but for fishing without rod, for instance sea-fishing for yachtsmen. Sometimes our nets were used for taking fish out of a river for transfer into another river or a pond or a reservoir. Sometimes a gamekeeper or a poacher would buy them off us. Quite often we made a special net for a customer to specification without knowing what it was for. This was not a main activity but over the years it brought us in quite a considerable sum, as did the catching of song-birds for pet shops and the odd orders for ferrets and rat-catching.

Nets and such things were just side lines. The seasonal work was the main thing. Cereals, root crops, beans, peas, lettuce, cabbage, soft fruit, apples, hops and other crops all had to be gathered in manually. Onions had to be hoed by hand with a short-handled hoe in each hand; you tended to lean on the left hoe and did most of the hoeing with the right. This was one of the jobs paid by the acre. Then there was the annual job of hedging—layering a hedge, cutting back without retarding or killing it, for which we had standing contracts with several landowners. Then there was ditching; clearing out; cutting land-drains with a rutter and hawk; laying drainpipes in trenches that we first lined with straw. Then there was a thing—a dying or dead craft—called wattle-hurdles; a sort of a basket or wicker-work type of gate or fence we used to make out of split hazel ends and chestnut. This was used for sheep pens, partitions for cattle in barns, to hold back straw and hay and sometimes for market garden fences.

We also did every kind of forestry work on private contract but never for local authorities of the Forestry Commission. In this field we were engaged mainly in thinning operations. This was on the whole the least profitable work we took on as we were paid by the amount of timber and firewood we managed to cut and stack without over-thinning. If you break the canopy of a wood, a copse or deep forest in a thinning operation and it does not fill in before the next storm a great many trees in the plantation will be twisted to the ground; so there is no chance of making up on bulk, or of rushing the job, on a thinning operation. But no matter how long the job takes there was a standard rate paid which was agreed from year to year on, say, a cord o' wood—which is a stack of firewood 8 ft 3in. wide by 4ft high by whatever depth you agreed on.

For years one of my uncles had a contract to repair the returnable drums for a paint factory. He had a special machine for turning new drum tops and new caps, new bottoms and handles. On most of the farms we were also regularly employed as knife and scissor grinders—mainly with a wet stone on a treadle-type machine. I was also employed in my own trade as a carpenter and joiner.

We also, as a tribe, did quite a lot of what the Gorgios tend to think of as traditional Gypsy crafts—peg-making and wooden flowers. I have seen several very good descriptions of how we used to make clothes pegs, so I won't repeat it here, but as far as I am aware wooden flower-making has never been described. The flowers were of the chrysanthemum type—of elderberry wood. The wood has a pith in the centre so you could insert a stem; you got the wood in long, straight pieces—any length—and you shaved the flower petals with a thin, sharp, leather cutter's knife. You shave off a long thin shaving by holding the knife firmly against your knee and drawing the wood towards you; the shaving curls up as you draw the wood along and you stop just short of the end of the stick and start from the bottom again

with the next shaving. As you draw the wood towards you, you keep turning it. Eventually the whole wood is turned into a lot of curly shavings growing out of the hollow centre and you can arrange them into a convincing looking chrysanthemum. Then the hollow centre is pierced with a bradawl and the flower is dyed. Finally privet stems are inserted in the centre and glued in. There used to be a very good sale for wooden flowers before the war but the bottom has been knocked out of the trade of recent years.

We also used to do a good trade in crepe paper roses dipped in wax, and some of the women did good lace-work, doylies and runners.

One year I was about to finish my travels towards the end of the autumn, when I was stopped on the road just inside Surrey on my way from Hampshire by a farmer who had employed me to put up some sheds in the past. He asked me if I would go on his farm and put up some rustic fencing, some new stable doors and quite a lot of other woodwork that needed doing around his farm. Well, we came to an agreement as to price and conditions—so I pulled onto his land with my wagon. This was the beginning of a lengthy stay—one of the most profitable I can remember—in which I not only worked for this farmer but also bred and sold a lot of ferrets, trained some local lads in ferreting, rid a number of farms of rats and other vermin, discouraged a plague of deer from entering an estate and tracked down and destroyed two foxes that kept raiding one of the local women's yards. Some of these jobs seem well worth describing here as they are a good illustration of the sort of skills Gypsies in the past had to acquire.

I'll skip the ferrets and the deer and go straight on to the foxes. A fox, like every other wild animal, has its accustomed run. If it regularly enters an estate it will always come in the same way and leave by the same exit. So I went to the woman's yard with my Jack Russell bitch to look for the foxes' tracks. The bitch soon picked up a scent which led away from the chicken house towards the boundary fence which was very thick with bracken, brambles and furze. I searched around in the brambles and bracken and found the boundary fence. The bitch soon found the run that the foxes had made—and in the wire fence there was a hole. I could see by the fine red hairs on the edge of the hole on the south side of the woman's land that this was part of the foxes' main run, and by the chicken feathers I could tell that this was the exit; from the great number of feathers I could tell that there was more than one fox using this run. On the north side of the land I found that the boundary fence was partly knocked down by a bough that had broken from an old oak. I could see by the marks in the earth each side of the fence that the foxes jumped the fence here. I had permission to go onto neighbouring land—which was as well, as further search revealed that the foxes came from quite a distance, only sometimes from the north, but more recently they apparently came mostly from the south and left by the north, as I could tell by the greater number of chicken feathers of more recent date at the northern end of the foxes' run. This change of habit was unusual but not unique.

To get these foxes I first had to warn the woman and her neighbours that I would put up some benders, which are special snares with trigger sticks, so that they would make sure that their dogs and pets would be kept away from the foxes' entry and exit points to the woman's land. Then I cut some young ash saplings to make my benders. I trimmed the saplings and made off for my camp. Back in the wagon I made two snares out of brake cable which I attached to two lengths of very strong sash-cord. Just behind each noose of the snares I fixed a two inch wire nail with a head into the cables. This was to go under the nails in the trigger-stick. The trigger-sticks looked like old-fashioned tent pegs of the sort used by the boy scouts. I cut them about a foot in length, pointed at one end and drove two oval nails in one edge, leaving the nails sticking out about half an inch. Then I cut the heads off the nails and filed them down. So there were two straight pointed sticks with two headless nails sticking out one edge.

I went straight back to the woman's place after my dinner and put up the benders. The most important thing when you do this is absolutely correct placing of the snares, the trigger-stick and the bender—or you will never get your fox. When you have made your mental calculations you must first secure the bender in the ground and fix the snare to it. Then you place the trigger-stick so that it will just hold down the bender by the two inch nail behind the snare. The nails in the trigger-stick must point away in the direction you expect the fox to run. When the bender and snare is lightly held by the trigger-stick you adjust the snare so that it will almost certainly ensnare and kill your fox. To get through the hole in the woman's fence the fox could only jump one way; its head would inevitably go through the noose, and the impact of the jump would jerk the cable off the trigger-stick or else pull the trigger-stick right out of the ground. This will make the bender fly up and break the fox's neck. The fox is killed instantly. Two things one has to watch when setting a bender; first, the trigger-stick and bent rod must be camouflaged, for instance, with bracken; secondly, it is advisable to tie a brightly-coloured piece of wool to the top of the bent rod, so you can see the top of the bender when the trap is sprung. If it is not sprung, you need not get too near and leave your scent behind on your daily checks.

I set the two benders, one at the north end and the other at the south end of the woman's land and went home for the day. That night I could hear the call of the vixen and the answer of the dog fox. I was up at six the next morning, called my Jack Russell bitch to heel right after breakfast and set off for the fox traps. As soon as I was near enough to the first trap I shone my torch over the braken and I could see the coloured wool on the sprung bender quite clearly. I went straight to the trap, and there, hanging up by the neck, was a dog fox. I touched him; he was dead and cold and I could see in the light of the torch that his neck was broken. Dawn was beginning to break when I got to the other trap. I had caught the vixen as well. What had happened was this: the vixen was just behind the fox when he was caught in the noose; she could not stop running, so she jumped onto the woman's land behind her mate and carried on in terror right across the woman's land and straight into the noose at the exit. This was the quickest operation of the kind in my experience. It sometimes takes days, or even weeks before you catch just one fox in this way. This success certainly boosted my reputation in that particular locality at the time.

The last type of activity I must describe to complete the picture of the old Romany ways of life is poaching. I suppose there are still quite a lot of poachers around—but I have not done any since about three years after the Second World War. Nowadays I have a shooting licence, an occasional fishing licence and sometimes even get asked to a hunt; so I have no need to go poaching any more. Also I seem to get less and less time for this sort of activity. But before the war we poached for anything and everything that was worth eating or skinning. We all believed that three things belonged naturally to all men: the wood that lies on the ground, the birds and beasts that live in the forest and on the heath and the fish in the water. These were all free for the taking and no man had any right to deny another the privilege of the taking. There were certain rules to be observed, of course—you would never go after game in the breeding season; you would never kill a beast under a certain size; you would try to catch unawares and painlessly. In these respects the old Romany poachers had the edge on all the other poachers who had no consideration at all for their quarry and used some very cruel and particularly destructive methods. What is more, I think we had a far more decent approach to this business of going after game than the gentry who hunt for fun. There is nothing funny in destruction and death—and while we certainly enjoyed the hunt as much as we knew how, we stopped when we had enough for the pot, or for our customers, and if we knew that game was scarce we did without.

As this is not a poaching book I will give only a few examples of how we worked. There was a disused part of a sand and gravel pit in Surrey just after the war which looked like a natural lake, having been flooded over the years. There were several small islands left in this lake and on one of these islands was a large horse-chestnut tree. You were able to wade there with a pair of waders. This lake used to be visited by hundreds of different kinds of wild ducks and geese, and when we were in this area in the right season in autumn we would wade out onto this island and build a hide-out of brushwood. We waited in this hide-out for the evening flight of ducks and geese to come in.

These birds included mallard, teal, widgeon, wild geese and a variety of other migratory birds.

We could hear the chattering of the ducks and the honking of the geese sometime before they flew over our guns. They would circle the lake three or four times, and each time they circled they'd be lower, until they got in the range of our guns. Then we could see them as they came between us and the neon lights which were on a far-off garage. We always tried to get a left and a right barrel at the ducks as we were using double-barrel twelve bores; but shooting at geese was a different matter. We would always let a flight of geese get by till the last one came into range. We always shot the last one so that the leading geese in the flight wouldn't see him fall. Doing it this way would not break up the flight of geese. If you shoot at them this way they'll turn and circle the lake again and you will be able to shoot at the next last one. But if you shoot one of the leaders in a flight of geese, the flight breaks up and they'll not come back. Ducks are different. They keep coming back. Our dogs were standing by ready to pick the birds out of the water. The dogs we used for this were crossbred spaniels. Cocker spaniel crossed with springer spaniel: crossed with labrador—springer spaniel—red setter.

When we had all the birds we needed we put them in a sack and made ready to leave. We waded out of the lake, climbed over a fence and onto the railway to hide the birds and the guns so that none of these things would be found on us so soon after the shooting. We put the guns in a sack with the dead birds and lowered the sack with a rope into a culvert to be collected the next day. We then climbed over the fence onto the footpath and split up. If there were just two of us, one of us would go over the stile straight back to the village while the other went in the opposite direction. This was done in order to give us a better chance of running into a bailiff, a policeman or a keeper on the way to the village. If either of us met any of them he could look very innocent and be very friendly. He could talk to them with a clear conscience as he had no gun and no game on him at all. He would ask the time of day and talk about the weather, and then get into conversation to find out if they knew that there were poachers about. Then, when we met up in the village we would decide on when to pick up our birds and guns.

When you go poaching the most important thing to watch is the movements of the keepers. As far as possible you will try to get your game noiselessly, with traps, snares, catapults or, in the case of pheasants, partridges and similar game-birds, with a whip consisting of a short stick with a long line and a weight attached. Such a whip you flick in a certain way so that the line wraps itself round the bird's neck. It just requires one quick jerk to kill the bird and one particular movement to unwrap the line and plonk the bird into your knapsack. A real good adept at this could almost bag a bird in this way while chatting with the keeper.

Poaching deer was almost like a military operation. For this we used a bow and arrow or sometimes an old flint-lock—what they call a muzzle-loader or a pushka—that was in my family then. We used to make our own candle-shot for this gun. Candle-shot is buck-shot and candle wax mixed together, so when the shot comes out at the end of the muzzle it is in one piece like a rifle bullet.

We knew the water holes that the deer used to drink from. We went up to clear one of those water holes out and then watched to see whether the deer came to drink in the evening or at night. Then we chose a hiding place and put up a cover of sticks and undergrowth to hide in. We lay in hiding with bow and arrow or flint-lock while one of the other lads lay somewhere close by with a double-barrelled shotgun which was used in case the deer wasn't killed outright. When the deer came to drink we selected one and shot it. The place we used to aim for was under the left shoulder of the deer—we always made for a heart shot—but if we missed the mark and the deer started to run, the lad with the double-barrelled gun dispatched it right away with both barrels.

Once we had shot our deer we cut the jugular vein and let it bleed—we pulled the hind quarters over the bough of a tree to bleed him and we secured him with a piece of sash-cord. To make sure that the keeper would not surprise us, one of us, further along in a different part of the forest, fired off blank cartridges from a very noisy gun to get the keeper to follow him on the wrong track and he kept moving away from the part where we were poaching the deer.

When the deer was bled we collected it and took its coat off. We put the meat in a sack which we hung up in a densely overgrown part of the wood to let it set so we could cut it up the next day.

Finally some favourite methods of poaching fish seem worth mentioning. The kindest way to get trout and salmon is by tickling. The fish apparently enjoys the sensation as much as a dog likes being stroked, and its death agony is reduced to a split second. You crawl to the river bank where you know a salmon or a trout is lying. You then slowly slide your hand into the water and under the fish and gently stroke its stomach just like you would stroke a pet animal; the fish will relax and rise up in the water towards the surface as you keep stroking it, and when it is near the surface you grab its tail and yank it out of the water onto the river bank.

Most other fish we caught with rod and line, but eels we got the way they catch lobsters—only in a sack instead of a pot. We used whelks, logworm, rotted liver or the paunch of a sheep in a sack with holes cut in it to catch eels. We put the bait into the sack and sewed it up. Then we cut small holes into the sack and pegged the whole thing down at the bottom of a stream where we knew that there were freshwater eels. We left this sack in the water all night and took it out the next morning. When we cut the top of the sack open we always found some eels that had gone in through the holes to get at the bait. A sheep's paunch was the best bait for this, worms were the worst bait—mostly they slipped from the sacking and went away.

This chapter by no means describes all the activities around an old Romany encampment but it gave a fairly representative selection of what can be put under the heading of work and play.

5   Of Devels and Bengs

Up till about a hundred years ago the Romany way of life was a complete system that was preserved almost intact all over Europe, the Middle East and Persia; so that any Romany could at any time fall in with any Romany tribe anywhere in the areas I mentioned. The whole system revolved around the language and the original Romany religion which, out of practical considerations, had to be blended with either the Christian or the Muslim faith, depending on which part of the world any particular tribe happened to travel. A lot of people seem to think that the Romany language was kept up merely as a secret tongue so that we could get away with all sorts of things that were on the wrong side of the law—but this is nonsense. For this sort of situation we would think up day-to-day codes either in English or in any other language we might be using at the time. For instance, we might refer to a chicken as a woman and say telling instead of stealing. Twist your language in a way people think they can understand and they will be far less suspicious of you than if you speak Romany. So, in this context, Romany would be more of a liability than an asset. The reason for keeping up with the language at all was purely practical. There were three branches of the language: there was the spoken word; there were the trail-signs—messages left in the shape of sticks, twigs, pebbles and so on, to show how many of a tribe had camped out in a certain place, with how many horses, donkeys, wagons, tents and so on, as well as whether the tribe were, say, musicians, metalworkers, or maybe horse-dealers; third, there was sign language and whistling signals that were all known to every Romany tribe. When a tribe travelled they also made a habit of leaving tufts of grass all along their route to show any of their friends which way they went.

Now language is without a doubt the greatest invention ever made by man. No other invention would have been possible without it because if we were unable to communicate our ideas and our discoveries these things would all die with us. Neither the wheel nor fire-making nor the bow would have got off the ground if the inventors of them had been unable to teach their mates and children about them. So it stands to reason that it is vital that a language should be held sacred by the people that speak it. Ideally neither the words nor the grammar of the language should undergo any change whatsover, and the pronunciation should always remain constant. Also the meanings of words should never be anything but what they were when they were first coined. This was particularly important with Romany because until fairly recent times the Romany race were all long-distance travellers who might trail into countries whose languages they could not speak. When that happened they looked out for trail-signs and hurried to catch up with their local prals who accepted them as soon as they had passed muster. They could then travel with that tribe and never have any language problems at all. In this way they could pass through a dozen countries with as many languages without having to learn a word of any language except for the language of the last country where they had some business to attend to. There they would link up with a local tribe until they were confident that they knew enough about local conditions and traditions to make their own way. If the language had become too corrupted in any of the countries of Europe or the Middle East or in Persia, the system would have broken down a long time ago. This has more or less happened today.

In order that the language should remain pure, each tribe had two or three story-tellers who were steeped in the Old Romany lore. There were said to be over a 1,000 stories that were memorized word for word and phrase for phrase by these story-tellers, and the tribes sat around the camp fires and listened to these stories and had them explained. About two thirds of these stories had to do with religion and ritual—but it was

Romany religion and ritual; so when any of the tribes took to religion, as the saying goes, that is, when they became evangelists and members of one or another of the churches, they stopped telling these particular stories and only kept on telling the other third that were just stories of no particular significance—and with that the language lost about half of its words. It was in fact the evangelists who knocked the first nails into the Romany coffin.

Now, as to Romany religion, there is not much anybody remembers of it today. There was a prophet called Soster and a lot of the stories had to do with him. This had mainly to do with magic—but I have never heard any of these stories, only of them. Fire was held to be sacred and was, along with water, considered the great purifier of anything that was ritually unclean. Originally the whole world was thought to be a complete nothingness—what the Gorgios would call a void—and within this void there was said to be another void. This smaller void was the sleeping god. It was all pure brain and it began to dream. The dream was an uncountable number of little sparks, and these little sparks all shot towards the centre where they gradually formed a huge ball of fire, which was whiter than white-hot and the pressure in the middle of it was gradually getting too great to bear—so it exploded and started to fly out in all directions at great speed, cooling on the way. So the brain of god grew and grew and its dream became the story of all our days. When the huge ball of fire blew up, two gods were born out of the explosion—the god of life, who was called Moshto; and the god of Death, called Arivell. Moshto had three sons; the eldest kept creating new life all the time; the second was a kind of service mechanic who busied himself with keeping the whole life-stream going by constantly balancing one part of the system with another; and the third son of Moshto was here to destroy any part of the system that endangered all the rest or was beyond repair, and was needed as raw material by the eldest brother to create new life with. The second son was the one held to be the most important of the three by the old Romanies— although he could not have done his job without the other two. The plant sacred to him was any kind of bean which was always supposed to be grown alongside any other crop in agriculture but never eaten. The reason for this is that beans attract some kind of small animal life to their roots that enrich the soil. It was thought that these small creatures lived off the waste products of the beans while the bean plants lived off the waste products of the small animals that cling to the roots of the beans. So both animals and plants profited from the deal and neither lost. But the combined waste products of both the beans and the small creatures that look like globules in the roots was many times what either of them required. So soil with a lot of beans in it will always be fertile whereas most other crops will impoverish it and will need to be manured with animal dung. But the Romanies were only agriculturists for perhaps a month in the year, if at all. The reason the second son was held to be the most important of the three was that he was a service mechanic and repairer, and that was what most of the Romanies were themselves. The eldest son of Moshto was the one held sacred by all the women because he was the god of fertility. But it was Moshto himself who was supposed to rule supreme and his sons only followed his instructions. Moshto was the god of life, of light, of fire. He was born out of the fire and his emblem was the camp fire flame on the green grassy ground under the blue sky—with either the sun or the moon and the stars gleaming overhead. You had to observe all his laws and to protect all the beneficial animals from harm and follow him through life. You also had to destroy all the harmful animals—the disease-carrying insects, rodents, cats and other parasites you came across because these were the creatures of the god of darkness, death and destruction—Arivell. He was not the same as Moshto's third son, who was a salvage man, preparing what he destroyed for further creation. No, Arivell was a poisoner who made deserts out of fertile land and who made water unfit for plants and fish to live in; and if ever he got the upper hand and the whole life-stream turned parasite, all life would come to an end and Moshto might never again be able to start it all off again. This, for what it is worth, is all that anybody, to my knowledge, can remember of the old Romany religion today.

The old Romanies rejected the one God, the creator of the universe, because he seemed an obvious, ridiculous invention to them. They said, 'A man can make a basket but a basket can't make a man. The reason for this is that a basket is inferior to a man and a man is more complicated than a basket. The Gorgios think that God must have created the world because the world is so perfect and complicated that it seems unlikely that it could have grown of its own accord. But if God had created the world He must have been a good deal superior to the world that he created—just like the man is superior to the basket he made—and if that is the case, how come that it was possible for God just to come into being while the world, which is inferior to him, could not?' To which the new evangelists, the Romany baptists and all the rest of them said 'Nonsense!—you're all nine parts dinilo!—if it was Moshto all the time and not Jehovah—how come that you are the only ones following him and that the world is still going on? And how come that the Christians and the Jews have all the gravy and you have generally only got their leftovers?' And this is why all the Romanies today have either become atheists or have taken to religion, and the old stories and the language have gradually died out—at least in this country. But a lot of the ritual and a lot of the superstitions connected with the old Romany religion still linger on—a different set in each tribe. So there are a lot of old customs that are definitely still going strong even among many of the evangelists. If you are clever enough you can interpret them all in the context of a belief in Moshto, his three sons and Arivell.

So, god, o puro devel, with the name of Moshto, includes everything in the whole world that supports life. He did not create the world. The world has always existed—first as a blank and then as a dream of the mother goddess of the universe. The devil, o puro beng, with the name of Arivell, is pledged to destroy life, and particularly man. Early on, according to the old story, the devil made a man and a woman out of clay but these were lifeless statues until Moshto came along and breathed life into them. To do this Moshto had to blow the seeds of the maidenhair tree—also known as a Gingko tree—into their mouths. This was the tree of life. As they became conscious they stood in front of two fruit trees—an apple tree in front of the woman and a pear tree in front of the man. The man ate a pear and the woman ate an apple—and these were the fruits of knowledge—but they had been put there by Arivell, the devil. With the eating of these fruits of knowledge they both lost their chance of everlasting life, but they knew how to mate with one another and to multiply. Their main task in life was to serve the plants around them—to spread their seeds to the far corners of the earth and to manure them. There were several stories dealing with this. One of them tells of the way man and the vegetarian birds and animals were meant to keep moving around, roaming the face of the earth, eating the fruits and nuts that are provided by the plants and trees as they go along. Man and the birds and animals were meant to keep moving around for this purpose. If they were meant to stay in one place they would all be rooted in the ground like a tree. The plants grow flowers and fruits which are supposed to attract the birds, the animals, and some insects. A man will take down a fruit, such as a pear and eat the whole of it. But one or two pips will go into his stomach whole and pass through his body. He will leave it a few miles further on with his droppings—which will provide the initial nourishment for when the pear tree first germinates. Other fruits and nuts will be scattered in a similar way by other feeders, like deer or horses or birds. When the plant is mature enough to flower, insects, like the honey bee, will come and germinate the flowers. Animals, birds and worms will keep feeding the plants with their droppings and the plants will keep feeding them with their fruits; some of the insects will fertilize the flowers and turn them into fruits, nuts and grain. But the devil, Arivell, the beng, is the enemy of them all and will try to destroy the lot.

He is responsible for the creation of parasites and disease. He also sends out nightmares and worries that bring on symptoms of the various diseases although you have not really got the diseases at all. Against this, Moshto, o puro devel, sends out the rider of the night. If, for instance, you have got warts— the real ones have a root like a setfast in a horse and have to be removed by surgery, but the ones brought on by nightmares or a troubled mind are just superficial, though they might grow into the real things; if they are superficial warts, they can be charmed away. If you believe in the rider of the night you need only say, 'Rider, rider, take away my warts!' and bed down with an easy mind, and within days your warts will disappear. If you don't altogether believe in the rider you will need to wear a charm that you believe in. Some will charm away a superficial wart by impaling a slug with a thorn. As the slug slowly pines away and shrinks so your superficial warts will disappear, but never a wart with a root. There are all sorts of other charms for a variety of sham diseases, but not a single one of these charms will ever work on the real thing. The rider of the night was supposed to come with the full moon and leave at the crow of a cock. This was the best time to make your saying and to work the charm— and within the month, your disease, or warts or other skin complaints would be gone, provided it was the type of thing that could be willed away.

The diseases were believed to have come about in the following way: to help and protect man, Moshto had created a race of good fairies, and the most beautiful among them was their queen, who lived in a crystal palace on the top of a granite mountain. But Arivell had created a demon people who lived in a dark cavern under the same mountain and who only came out into the open on very dark nights, and he ordered them to subdue the fairies if they could. The king of the demons went up to the palace in which the queen lived to introduce himself and propose marriage to her, as this would have been the simplest and quickest way to get control of her and her people, but when she saw him she was so horrified by his appearance that she fainted. While she was in her swoon he explored the palace and found a secret passage to the outside through which he let in the rest of his demons who went about killing and eating quite a lot of the fairies—so when the queen came to she agreed to marry the king of the demons on condition that the rest of her people would be spared. But the queen found her husband so repulsive that she could not give herself to him, and so he had to drug her whenever he wanted to make love to her. Each time he made love to her she bore him a demon that was more terrible than the king was himself. The old story gave a whole long list of demons with their names, that were the children of the queen of the fairies and the king of the demons, what they looked like, and what diseases they represented. Some of them spread epidemics of terrible diseases like the plague; some just gave people they came in contact with a thick head. I don't suppose anybody still remembers the whole of the old tale—which is a pity as it deals with magic, fairies, demons, medicine and sex, and there are not many stories that contain all these things. The only demon-child of the demon and the fairy that I can remember is one, I don't know the name, that had the body of a fish with a man's head; the head had a beard of nine long sticky hairs on each cheek, and if he went past you, these sticky hairs would go right through you and give you a catarrh.

    To avoid getting in contact with these various disease-demons you had to keep up strict rules of ritual clean-liness. You had to avoid doing certain things and you had to attempt to keep away from any animals that were considered unclean or mokada. Dogs and cats are both mokada—dogs only up to a certain point, cats altogether—in fact, the cat is the most unclean animal there is, even more so than a rat; it used to be considered unspeakably dirty and a harbinger of death, if a cat got into your tent or your wagon you had to go through a purification ceremony—and I hear that this was still the custom at the turn of this century. Dogs were never considered as dirty as cats—you handled them all the time—but they were not allowed inside a wagon or tent. They were made to sleep under the wagon near where the harness was kept. But no horse was ever thought of as mokada; nor a donkey; nor a goat; nor a cow; nor a mule; nor most birds. Some of these were almost considered as a part of the family. But cats and rodents you were not supposed to touch at all if you could avoid it. Dogs you could handle as much as you liked but you were never allowed to let them lick your face, or to touch your face with your hands if they had been in contact with your dog until you have washed them. A dish used by an animal could never be washed in the same basin as a dish from which you had your own food; and you could not wash your cup or your cutlery in the same basin as you used for, say, your dog's dish. In fact everyone was supposed to have his own cup, saucer, knife, fork, spoon and plate, and strictly speaking, in the old Romany way each one's dishes and cutlery were supposed to be washed separately. At any rate, men's and women's things were supposed to be washed up separately at the very least. A basin that was used for washing yourself in could never be used for dishes. That would be extremely mokada. And there would be a different basin again for washing clothes in. In very strict families there would be a different basin for men's clothing and for women's clothing. And a man was never allowed to walk under women's clothes on the line.

As to food, there are some animals that you could never eat because it is mokada. A fox is a mokada-jook—a dirty dog, in other words, and you could never eat him; nor a cat; nor a rat; in fact not any beast of prey or bird of prey, vulture, raven or crow. In the old days, according to the stories, you were never supposed to kill any animal at all for food except when there was a shortage of other food; then you were allowed to kill anything with bristles—the wild boar, or the domestic pig or a hedgehog—and any animal with antlers, but positively nothing else. You were only supposed to live on fish, fruit, nuts and vegetables. Any meat you had in normal times had to be carrion that was cured over a certain period with salt and saltpetre. When this was cured to the required time it had to be cooked for several hours before it was declared pure. This has been discontinued many years ago and I don't know of any Romany today whose grandparents still ate carrion—or who did not hunt any animals they took a fancy to. A hedgehog you were never supposed to kill at all in the old Romany way unless there were plenty of hedgehogs in the area. This had to do with the hedgehog being thought of as one of the creatures of Moshto, the god of life. The hedgehog has an antidote in its system against most animal and plant poisons; it is supposed to be immune to the deadly nightshade; and it will go for an adder or a viper and kill it with a bite on the spine and then eat it—poison sacks and all. The hedgehog will eat every kind of garden-, farm- and forest-pest, and it should not be destroyed at all unless there are a good many of them in the area. But when you do kill one you will find that its flesh is out of this world. Its fat is one of the best ointments there is.

71

It is to this day thought mokada by a lot of Romanies for a man and a woman to use the same dishes or cutlery. One of the Scamp women once told me that she has a very special relationship with her husband—whenever they go into a transport café they drink from opposite sides of the same tea cup; well, before the war this would have been unthinkable among the Romanies. You could never have drunk out of a brook or a well or a trough after a dog had been drinking from it—but you could drink after a horse if it was in a fit condition; but you and your monishi could never drink out of the same cup; you each had your own dishes and there was one set spare in case you entertained Gorgio visitors—Romany visitors were supposed to bring their own cups, plates and cutlery. Another thing you could not do was to drink water from a brook or any container —such as a pail—if a woman had stepped over it. In the case of the brook—this would be mokada for several hours; a well or a trough would not be clean for days; and the water in a pail could only be used for washing women's clothes in if a woman had stepped over it. If this woman had stepped over any dish, cup or foodstuff this would automatically be declared as mokada. The utensils would have to be destroyed and the food either thrown out or given to the dogs or ferrets. Another thing was that if you found a bluebottle or a greenfly in your food, or a hair, either human or animal—the food had to be thrown out at once. In that case the food was not even to be fed to the dogs but was supposed to be buried. While on the subject of hairs, in the old days no Romany woman was ever allowed to undo her hair and comb it while a man was present. She could only do her hair when she was alone or in the presence of other women and girls. The women had a pretty thin time of it altogether in the old-fashioned Romany households. In some households they could argue as much with their men as they liked, as long as they were alone, but they had no right to make a peep if any strangers were present. When any man was around, the unmarried women and girls had either to stand or to sit cross-legged on the floor, though the married ones could sit with their legs straight out but tightly pressed together—even if the only man around was her husband, her father, or her son. This kind of rule has not been observed by anyone that I know of for a good many years—just a few of the older ones a few years before the war still stuck to this. Another rule for women that is now gradually disappearing is that she must never pass in front of a sitting man—always behind him; she can pass or face a standing man, but never a sitting man. At night he is supposed to get into bed first and sleep nearer the wall, and at daybreak she is supposed to rise before him. These rules, and the one that no man may walk under a clothes line with women's washing on it, have all to do with women's internal bleeding during her periods—the blood from this is most mokada. But a female child is never thought of as mokada right until her periods first come on. Her washing could be hung up with the men's. In fact, no distinction was ever made between boys and girls up to the age of about twelve or thirteen—except in the sort of jobs they were taught. But once a woman got into her periods she was not supposed to cook, or even touch any food except her own—she had to ask somebody else to do the kitchen work for her. And that was the way one could always tell she had her period—because she was never supposed to mention that particular ailment to anyone. But most of these old rules are on the way out. Only those rules that are the same in the traditional Christian customs are still going strong.

Now, the first Gypsy to give up all the old beliefs and become a Christian was Saint Sarah who was the chief of her tribe going around in France. At the time she had a vision of three saints who would arrive by boat near the mouth of the river Rhone and would need her help to reach the land. She got up and walked to the spot that was indicated in her vision and arrived just in time to see the boat arrive in a very rough sea. So she took off her cloak and threw it on the waves and it floated. So she stepped onto the cloak and used it as a raft which floated over to the saints, who joined her just before their boat foundered. With the one remaining oar of the boat they managed to reach land in safety. The saints baptized Sarah who became their maidservant. She converted all of her tribe to Christianity because of her miracle, and since then more and more Gypsies have become more or less Christian. Since the Evangelists—and particularly the Baptists—have moved into the act, more and more Gypsies have become Protestants, though there are still plenty of Catholics around too. Saint Sarah is known as Sarah the Kali or Black Sarah and the three Saints whose servant she was, were Mary Salomy, Mary Jacoby and Mary Magdalene, who had all been present at the death of Jesus some hundreds of years before they landed in France.

Now, with going over to Christianity, the old stories were to a great extent scrapped, and also a lot of the language, but a new lot of Romany tales started being told in the place of the old ones. One of them is the story of the wooden horse shoe and the three nails.

There was once an innkeeper who traded in horses, donkeys and mules. One year the Romans conquered the land and built roads. The horse's hooves suffered a great deal of wear and tear as a result of going over the hard surface of the roads instead of the sandy dunes as hitherto. One night the inn-keeper's son brooded over the problem and it occurred to him that it should be possible to fit wooden clogs onto the horse's hooves. So the next day he carved some wooden horseshoes out of cedar wood—but these were not very durable.

Some weeks after making the first wooden horse-shoes the innkeeper's son had a dream—he dreamed of a way of forging iron horseshoes, and within a month the first smithy in the world was built. The innkeeper's son was the first smith and he shoed horses and made nails for the whole world.

One day, when the smith was already very old, a man came to him and ordered the twelve large nails with which Jesus and the two thieves were to be nailed to the cross; but after having delivered nine of the nails, he found out what these nails were to be used for and so he withheld the other three nails.

One of the executioners came round to the smithy to get the other three nails, and a search party came with him; but one of the smith's sons had managed to escape with these three nails, and so the gentiles never managed to find them and the crucifixion had to be managed with nine nails only, three for each of the condemned. The saying goes that the gen-tiles have been looking for the missing three nails ever since and it has been this constant search for them that has led to the persecution of the Gypsies. If ever these nails are found the persecution will come to an end. But if they are not found soon, the Gorgios will kill each other off by being too clever by half and only the Gypsies and other wandering people will survive the holocaust.

Anyway, to return to the tale, Christ and the two thieves were crucified with only three nails each—two through the wrists and one through both feet—and after the crucifixion the citizens of the town formed themselves into a lynch mob and went to string up the smith and all his friends and relations, because they had delivered the nine nails used for the crucifixion; but the smith and all his lot had managed to make a getaway, and have been hounded from place to place ever since.

The smith was condemned to eternal life. On bright nights you can see him sitting on the moon with his hammer in his hand, his anvil by his side and other tools of his trade scattered around him.

One of the smith's sons managed to conceal his identity and marry a princess. Her father, the king of Romania, went blind because of the curse on the smith's family. The smith's son went in search of a magic herb grown by a magician belonging to his tribe. But he was waylaid by the king's three sons who nailed a red hot horseshoe on his backside and branded its imprint deep into his skin, However, the smith's son recovered from this torture and procured the magic herb. The king was cured of his blindness and he should have been grateful to the smith's son, but he banished him from the country instead when his daughter, the princess, told him about the mark branded on her husband's backside. However, he did not banish any of the smith's people from the country—partly because they were clever herbal doctors and partly because they forged very good weapons for his army. Only his daughter's husband was banished for making a fool of him and his royal house. So the smith's descendants stayed in Romania for many centuries and that is why they are to this day known as Romanies, and their way of life is called roaming or roving.

Now, to finish this chapter of stories, customs and

superstitions I would like to deal with some peculiar attitudes to names. Very occasionally in the old days Romanies called their children after flowers, fishes, trees or animals. If anybody with the name of, say, a flower died, this flower was never to be mentioned by that name again in the family for a period of years—so a new name had to be found for it for whatever period was fixed. So there used to be a name Shoshoi for either a rabbit or a hare; (bawro shoshoi or hashoi for a hare; bitta shoshoi for a rabbit). This word Shoshoi was for some reason used a lot as a Christian name two hundred years ago in England—so the word went out of use for rabbit and hare, and rabbit became shoshi and hare became morgan, and finally they both got all sorts of other names, like drummer for a rabbit and kanengri or kanengro for a hare, and so on. After the period for which the word was never to be mentioned everybody had got so used to the temporary code word that the real word came out of use.

There are some travellers, mainly Didikais, who go by a different name in every locality they work in their circle. Some will just keep a different Christian name, others will go by a different Christian and surname in different places, or even with different people in any one place. The reason for this is not clear to me—they are not criminals on the run or anything like that, they are not even trying to conceal anything; they just keep different names for different places and people they deal with quite regularly and openly, working or doing business. Further, while I am on this subject, I know a family where the father's name is Smith, the mother's name is Cooper, and I have known three children in that family who went to school with me, and one of them went in the name of James, one went to school in the name of Lee and the other went in the name of Boswell. Also I have known in the Brasil family—some went to school in the name of Brasil and some in the name of Warris and a sister went in the name of Green; and in a lot of other Romany families they used to christen one child in one name and the next in another—but why they did this I really don't know. It was never done in my family at all and it was never done in our tribe; only when trouble came our way that could not be settled in the normal fashion, as we could not trace who was responsible in the first place, did it come in handy to have another name for a few minutes to save time. My family in particular were not very often in trouble with the law. But there were a few rare occasions when I heard the name 'the Charwood', mentioned. Now we took our name from wood because we were woodworkers. But at one time—and the first time was on Hayes Common—something had happened that had nothing at all to do with us, really—it concerned somebody else—but the police had stopped us on the road and they asked, was our name Wood? And my uncle said, 'No, our name isn't Wood, it is Charwood.'

My uncle and my grandfather never, at any time, had to use another name; but if they had used their own name on this particular occasion and a few other times like it—when the people that the police were after had used our name to get us into trouble and at the same time escape from the law, so my uncle and my grandfather used somebody else's name, a small Gypsy tribe's who got their name because they burned charcoal and who were never anywhere near to our various routes. If we would have said that our name was Wood, we would have had to go to the police station, and this would have caused us a lot of inconvenience as we might have been held over night and come up before the magistrates the next day on God knows what charge. Even if the case was dismissed—if the magistrates believed us, which seems unlikely—we would have made a point of stopping in the area to get to the bottom of things and get our name cleared. So we did use the name Charwood on a few occasions because it was simpler.

This chapter, of course, only gives a brief summary of old beliefs and customs. Much could have been said, in addition, in connection with the customs of child-birth. Traditionally, a woman had to go through labour and the birth of her child in a special tent that was burned with all its contents as soon as she and her child had moved back into the wagon. Other points—a list of taboos of things that must never be done in a wagon, and items that must not be brought into the wagon—could fill a book; but it would merely be a list of customs for which there is no explanation.

6   The Old Witch's Cauldron

According to an old tradition, all medicine started with cooking. You must know what to put into the pot, the right order of the ingredients and how long you must leave the pot on the boil between ingredients.

In the old Romany stew you first fried meat and potatoes together and when they were nearly done you added plenty of onions, and then topped the lot with boiling water and plenty of herbs. Fresh herbs were always preferred to dried herbs. Add some greens with the herbs and take the pot off the boil very soon after that, so that the greens were still nice and crisp when you chewed them. With this kind of stew you would very often have a gooey of one kind or another. This is sometimes a dumpling, sometimes a pudding, sometimes a pie. One favourite gooey was made of oatmeal, goose's blood and suet— pounded together in that order. This was at one time known as pussani gooey. I have not had anything like that in many years.

Another favourite gooey was cheriloe's gooey or sparrow's pie. Let your sparrows lie for at least three days after you have killed them. Then you must pick them and clean them, put them in salt water for at least twelve hours and wash them. Boil them until the flesh will leave the bone. Take the flesh from the bone, put it on a clean plate, and then prepare the dough as you would for an ordinary chicken pie. Sparrow's pie is made in a pie dish in the same way as any other pie. It is best eaten cold with grated carrot and chickweed salad and sorrel, or with fresh mint and a sprinkling of freshly gathered lime blossoms. You need at least a dozen sparrows to go into a pie.

Another favourite animal for the pot used to be a

hedgehog. To catch a hedgehog you put your foot on its back and gently roll it from side to side until it has unrolled. You must exert just enough pressure with your foot in the middle of the hedgehog's back for this. When it has unrolled you pick it up by one of its hind legs and take off the tip of its nose with a sharp blow from a stick. This kills it instantly and allows the blood to drain off. You will find that it is full of fleas. These you burn off with the bristles, either by hanging your hedgehog on a kettle-prop with a piece of wire and burning around it with a taper, or by just rolling the hedgehog in a roaring fire. When you have got the bristles off, you take a sharp knife and stick it in the back of the head and fetch the knife right over the hedgehog's back, and skin it as you would a rabbit. Then you can lay it in salt water or cook it straight away—though with all these things—sparrows, hedgehogs and so on, you must make sure that only the clean parts of the animal go into the dish. With a hedgehog I always get a stick, sharpen it like a skewer and stick it right through the whole length of the hedgehog for roasting over the open fire. There is a forked stick in the ground and the skewer-stick lies across this; the skewer-stick is held in position by a length of string pegged into the ground. You keep turning it every so often. A dish on the side catches the fat as it drips out of the hedgehog. In the old days hedgehogs were packed into clay and baked slowly on an open charcoal fire until the clay was hard—eggs were sometimes baked in the same way if you had a lot of them and wanted to preserve them for an indefinite period, up to several years if the clay remained unbroken—but nowadays the method is no longer used. The trouble with baking in clay is that you have to be careful to do it hot enough, but not too hot. If you had it too hot, your egg or your hedgehog exploded on you. But if you did manage to bake your hedgehog in clay, you had something very neat and superior in taste. When the clay was hard enough, you cracked it at the belly side of the hedgehog, and all the skin, paws and bristles came off with the shell. Then you continued as with a skinned hedgehog.

A lot of the old Romanies would not use hedgehog fat for cooking, as it is of great medicinal value. It—and the blood of the hedgehog also—contains antidotes against a great number of poisons; this enables the hedgehog to eat almost anything that moves. In any case, hedgehog fat is quite definitely an effective treatment for anybody who has a skin complaint, a boil or dandruff. It is also very good for fetching the hard skin off the bottoms of your feet and it is a good cure for mange on a dog. For maybe fifteen or twenty different complaints you will find that hedgehog fat is the finest thing out for a certain cure—and that's a fact!

This brings us from cookery to natural medicine. What you put in the pot is partly medicine and partly food. A lot of fat—including hedgehog fat—in your food is bad for you; so the Romany cook cuts it out as far as possible. The fat parts were sometimes used externally for skin troubles, boils and rashes. But if you did have some very rich food in the pot and you did not have time to remove the grease—or if you had some very fat bacon—you always put a lot of onion, garlic, or both with it. In fact, if anybody had blood-spots showing on his skin, or if he got an occasional stroke, he was supposed to take plenty of onions with his food.

Onions were also thought of as being a good disinfectant for the mouth if you chewed them raw—good for colds and sore throats—but they had the snag of bringing on all sorts of new symptoms, as they have a burning effect on your gums, tongue and throat, which in turn has to be treated with, among other things, cold black tea and carrots. Onions for the complaint that nowadays is called coronary thrombosis can be taken either raw, minced, fried or boiled, and the more you take—up to a pound a day—the less likely you are to get an attack. If you cannot take onions, the closely related vegetables—like chives and leeks—will have some beneficial effect. Some Romanies even fed a certain amount of onions to their horses—mixed into the feed—as this was supposed to prevent blood clots in the legs—but we never did anything like that in our family.

Another favourite cure-all of the hedgehog and onion class was raw honey. This substance was bought in small quantities from bee-keepers direct, as the stuff sold in the shops had its curative powers destroyed by heat-blending. Raw honey has a lot of crystals and bits of wax, or even part of a honeycomb in it, and it is exactly as the bees made it. It will cure dozens of minor ailments such as burns, ant bites and nettle rash, but it would not generally be wasted on such complaints. It was used as a cure for cholera, typhoid and dysentry but its most important use was for bad cuts and gashes; all you had to do was to put a generous helping of raw honey on the wound and cover the honeyed wound with gauze, and bandage up. The honey will both clean and heal the wound in record time.

A cure I am often asked about is mandrake, a plant that grows here and there in this country. A young mandrake root is like a parsnip to look at; but the top is not like a parsnip at all; the top is a vine that runs and makes a small flower. When the mandrake becomes an adult plant it takes on the shape of a man or a woman—it has a body with a head, arms, legs, fingers and toes—exactly like men and women in every way. The male sends out his feelers and his vines and they will travel all over the ground and run a long, long way—it might take several years—until he comes in contact with a female. When they contact each other and their vines intertwine, the male and female plants will move through the ground until they come close to each other. Then they will mate in the same way as humans do.

I have dug up mandrake plants when they were in the act of mating. Years ago when I was a small lad certain people used to come to my father with an order for mandrake. These were itinerant herbalists and they came to us because we were the only people in the area who knew where mandrake grew. The herbalists bought the mandrake off us and hawked it around the various pubs where they sold it in small cuttings for people to chew, as mandrake is very good for chest troubles, but you have got to know the way to compound it—if you use it the wrong way it can be very dangerous, which is probably the reason why the selling of mandrake in pubs has been discontinued of recent years. But before the war, when I was a lad, we did quite a big business selling mandrake to those pub-crawling herbalists.

Another favourite cure for a number of serious

ailments was the dandelion. Liver complaints, kidney complaints, jaundice, dropsy and so on, are all helped by eating dandelion leaves. In the spring, the washed, tender leaves taste very similar to lettuce except that they tend to be a little more bitter, although not as bitter as chicory; but dandelion is much better than either lettuce or chicory in purifying the blood. The juice from the stem is very good for curing warts. The only trouble with it is that it stains your hands and everything else that it touches.

Very often, even in the past, a Romany would call in a Gorgio doctor in extreme cases, but even when he did call in this Gorgio doctor he would also apply his own remedies. The old remedies were not thought to clash with the new. In this connection a letter from a retired G.P., Dr Tudor Edmunds, M.B., B.Sc., to John Brune, acting temporary clerk to the Gypsy Council at the time, seems worth quoting here:

For a number of years there was a Gypsy encampment near the town where I was in general practice, and so from time to time I was called in to attend to one or the other of them when they were ill.

On the first occasion I was rather worried because the man in question had a severe wound of the hand which had been caused by some dirty instrument, and he was living in very primitive surroundings in a hut in a field.

I naturally expected septic complications, but was interested, and quite relieved to find that the wound healed very quickly with no complications.

As time went on it was borne in on me that they all had a high resistance to disease, with great recuperative powers when illness did occur.

I remember an elderly man with acute pneumonia (before the days of antibiotics.) He was extremely ill, in his primitive hut made of tin boxes, linoleum and canvas, and I felt his chances of recovery were almost nil. In *three* days, however, he was up and about, and simply a little weak, though he said he was quite well once more, and in fact had no relapse or other complication!

One can only surmise that the hard open-air life has killed off all the weak strains, leaving only the tough and robust elements to perpetuate their race.

Well, I doubt Dr Edmund's conclusion—the death rate in the encampments was, if anything, lower than among the Gorgios; and once any of our people take to the Gorgio way of life they are generally less tough and robust than their Gorgio neighbours. So the answer is probably that the old way of life and the old cures are more effective in keeping you in fine fettle.

In the old days among Gypsies, cooking and making up cures was woman's work; surgery and treating animals was man's work. I learned most of what I know about cures from my grandmother, who only gave away the most common remedies to any of the men and boys in the tribe. My grandmother learned how to prepare her various concoctions from her grandmother and they were all very old cures known to Romanies and sometimes to country people as well. My grandmother used to spend weeks and weeks in every year making these things up in jars for use in the tribe and also for sale.

The art of prescribing the right medicine right away by asking the right questions when some outsider came to you for help played a very important part in the upbringing of a number of girls in every Romany tribe in the past. This was a very profitable business in many country districts where the Romany herbalists were very much cheaper to consult than the local doctors.

Here is a sampler with the odd stories that come to mind on what went into the old witches cauldron:

Common cold. A tea is made out of equal parts of dried elder flowers, peppermint and yarrow. Another good tea was prepared with equal parts of woodsage and ground ivy. For just a chill you used stinging nettles boiled down till the liquid looked like tea.

Sore throats. The juice of honeysuckle berries made into lozenges was taken for this, but you had to be very careful as to the right, safe quantities. In the season you boiled a small amount of wild rye or way-bennet in water and drank the liquor as a tea. Stick-wort tea was also used.

Bronchitis. Smoke dried leaves of laughwort or coltsfoot as a herbal tobacco. There are also four types of tea for bronchitis: marshmallow root tea, madweed tea, cuckoopint flower tea and cuckoopint root tea. The root of the cuckoopint, or wake-robin, is probably the best thing for bronchitis. The root is sliced up very finely and is boiled in water for up to half an hour. The liquor is then allowed to cool and bottled. It is taken in small quantities several times a day.

Asthma. Smoke a herbal tobacco made up of dried dandelion leaves and eyebright leaves. If you needed something stronger you smoked a mixture of dried dandelion leaves, coltsfoot, parsley, sage, lavender, rosemary and thyme. This mixture was also used for all sorts of other bronchial and lung complaints. Lavender, incidentally, was generally used to keep moths from your woolens.

Pneumonia. Put the patient into bed and keep him very warm, and in the bedroom—usually a small bender tent put up specially as a sickroom—they used to have two or three kettles steaming all the time to make the air soft so the patient could breathe better. These kettles stood on small stoves outside the tent with their spouts steaming into the tent through small holes. The stoves were covered outside with special porches. The kettles were kept steaming all the time, night and day and the women in the family took turns nursing the patient until he, or she, was out of danger. They used to hot up clean flannels in the oven and put them on the patient's chest and back while another flannel was waiting in the hot oven. These flannels would be changed at regular intervals.

My mother and my grandmother were complimented many times for their skill and perseverence in breaking the disease. I remember one particular time when I was very young—my father was sitting up all night with a horse out in the field because the horse was very ill. He caught pneumonia and pleurisy. In his sick-bed he became delirious and talked about the Germans riding through Flanders, the Angels of Mons, and he could see Jesus falling off the Cross. When my mother and grandmother heard mention of Jesus falling off the cross they quickly sent for the Scots doctor up the road. He said to my mother that she had nothing to worry about as my father was getting the best nursing anywhere in England and that the nine-days'-crisis was coming to an end. My father just raved on about his wartime adventures— he was a rough rider, a bareback rider taking despatches through the enemy lines, and he was mentioned in despatches. Once he was with a party in No-Man's-Land—they were all killed, but he was behind the enemy lines for three weeks with a horse, and he kept himself and the horse alive until he could finally make his way back to our lines. Through this and through the information he was carrying he was mentioned in despatches. He relived it all in his delirium. This did not frighten my mother and my grandmother, but when they heard my father mention Jesus falling off the Cross they thought he was certainly dying—so they sent for the doctor, and if they had been Catholics they would certainly have sent for a priest as well.

Some time after my father had got over this particularly bad attack of pneumonia, my mother, my grandmother and I were on a pony and trolley and we were travelling through Mitcham on our way to Streatham where my grandmother had some orders for flowers. We met one of the Cooper women on the way—Alice Cooper—a member of a very old Romany tribe who at this time were stopping in Mitcham, in a place called Redskin Village. She said her husband was very ill with pneumonia. So after we had made our deliveries we drove over to Redskin Village to see old Cooper. He was lying in bed with a breast of mutton tied to his feet. This was supposed to drive the evil spirits out of his body. If my grandmother had not gone over there he would have died, as a person who suffers from pneumonia has to be kept warm. Some Romanies used to swear that 'flu could be frozen out—keep you temperature down and shiver for a night and the disease will die on you—but for pneumonia the opposite treatment is essential at all times.

Fevers. There are a number of ways to reduce fevers. Use blackberry leaves as a herbal tobacco. Boil down dog grass, twitch grass or couch grass into a syrup and take cold. Take an infusion of dried cowslips in water—the cold liquor. An infusion of dried leaves of foxglove can also be taken—cold or warm. Several other infusions were used including those of sticklewort and dittany or wood-sage.

Cancer. We used to make a poultice of the leaves of violets— we put them in boiling water and put the leaves hot on what appeared to be cancerous growths; we also got people to drink the liquor of the leaves for internal cures of such growths. If the growths were benign the treatment worked and the growths never became malignant; but if the growths were malignant the treatment did not work. It was a true belief of the Romany people that this treatment could cure cancer.

Skin complaints. Most of these complaints can be avoided by eating plenty of fresh vegetables as salad. Chickweed eaten in your salad is particularly good; also carrots; also young stinging-nettles boiled down into a mock-spinach. For prickly heat and similar rashes—to purify the blood—take an infusion of marsh trefoil, buckbean or bogbean leaves. Fresh leaves are best, but dried leaves will do some good too.

Baldness. To prevent baldness, nettles are gathered in July and dried; heather seeds must be gathered and dried in the second week of September—in exceptionally hot years, the week before. From October onwards equal parts of dried nettles and heather seeds must be brewed in a pot of water for twenty minutes. The liquor is strained off and bottled. It is rubbed into the scalp every night after washing the head in warm water with a dash of cider vinegar in it. Hedgehog oil and a lotion made from St John's wort are used in the same way.

Warts. Deep warts can often only be removed by surgery. Superficial warts can be shifted by a number of plant juices, or by charms which will work provided you believe in them, or by a combination of the juices and one or the other charm. Two favourite juices are the juice of celandine and the juice of the stem of a dandelion.

Piles. An ointment is made from juice of the fresh leaves of coltsfoot—either obtained fresh by pressing out in a screw-press, or boiled down in water or unsalted lard. Another ointment was prepared from the pilewort. There were several other ointments made up, as well as an infusion of pilewort which, taken four times a day, cured the complaint in four or five days.

But the thing by which most Gypsies swore was sweet chestnuts for piles. The nuts are baked, boiled or roasted until they are hard. They are then powdered and made into a poultice. Some preferred to take off the soft shells and the skin around the nuts, dry the raw nuts and then powder them up for the poultice. Others used the powdered nuts on bread and ate them—this also seemed to work. Others again wore a chestnut sewn into a small bag round their necks as a charm against piles. But the bag was never of silk as this would have been very unlucky and brought on piles instead of preventing them.

Boils. One way of drawing out a boil is by tying some fat portion of bacon with a hole in it over it; the hole in the bacon must be placed exactly above the head of the boil. This is a good method if the boil is on your arm or hand. For a boil on the back of your neck the best thing is a bread poultice. Take some bread, soak it in water and put it in a piece of muslin, tie it up with string, put it in a tin and pop it into the oven until is it quite hot. You let the bread poultice get as hot as you can bear and then apply it to the boil. You must always keep enough water in the tin to have a fairly soggy bread poultice. This treatment is very painful but after several attempts it will draw the boil right out.

I remember some years ago, one of my uncles had a boil at the back of his neck and he would not let anybody touch it. So while he was sitting down in the wagon entrance one afternoon looking out, carving an ornamental head for a local antique and art dealer, one of my aunts got some lard—this is another cure for boils—she got some lard, a good big lump of it, and wrapped it in two layers of muslin which she tied up with string. She popped this lot into a tin in the oven. When she thought that the larded muslin was hot enough, she picked it out of the tin with two clothes pegs, crept up behind my uncle and popped the hot muslin straight on the boil on the back of his neck. It was almost red hot and he passed right out—and so did his boil!

Toothache. You can reduce the pain by sucking the baked foot of a hedgehog. You can also apply a mixture of the juices of the roots of a daisy and ginger. Cloves or chewing tobacco also help—but the only cure is to have the tooth out or filled by a dentist.

Canker in the mouth. For this, raw honey or the berries of the honeysuckle are both effective.

Worms. To expel worms you can take an infusion of the flowers and leaves of the lesser bindweed; or you slice the roots of bracken and boil them for twenty minutes to half an hour in water. Mix the strained liquor with red wine and take three times a day. Or you take an infusion of the crushed leaves and shoots of broom—and this will do the trick inside a fortnight. An infusion of tansy flowers will do the trick in a matter of days.

Diarrhoea. A small dose of polypore in some cases effects a complete cure. Another treatment was crushed root of wild rye, clove root or colewort, which, taken in small quantities, will bring you back to normal.

Constipation. The berries of the black or buckthorn alder were used in very small doses; this is one of the most powerful purgatives and can be dangerous. A milder purgative is produced by boiling the bark of the black alder for about half an hour and drinking the strained liquor.

It is amazing how different barks will react to boiling—the bark of a holly tree will give you a water-resistant glue if it is boiled down with a particular other ingredient; on its own it will give you bird-lime. Other barks will give you a permanent dye, and others again a useful medicine for one complaint or another. My grandmother used to collect about thirty different kinds of bark wherever we went—mostly for treatments and cures of various complaints.

Anaemia. Drink stinging-nettle tea.

Expectant Mothers. They used to drink a lot of linseed tea to have an easy birth.

Jaundice. You keep off fatty foods, meat, fish, eggs and dairy foods. You eat only a little light food and fresh vegetables half cooked. There are various tonics made: feverwort or Christ's ladder infused in water is one; the liquor of the root of wild chicory boiled down in hot water for about half an hour is another—there are a good dozen others.

Dropsy. The main ingredients for dropsy cures are the same as for liver and kidney complaints. The most popular cures use the juice of the dandelion root in one form or another. The simplest remedies are dandelion tea, stinging-nettle tea and a very weak infusion of sliced roots of meadow saffron.

Rheumatism. Rheumatism was a common complaint. Some of this was imagined and was best cured with an imaginary cure that did wonders. The bogus embrocation was a mixture of equal parts of milk and paraffin. This looked and smelled very convincing as an embrocation. It was also quite harmless. For the real complaint there is an embrocation of kelpware and hot water—in chronic cases hot whisky, which is one of the finest reliefs there is.

Broken Bones. Broken bones are set and then bound with knitbone, nipbone, blackwort or comfrey which helps to speed up healing. But, of course, this was done only in addition to the normal way you would deal with a fracture in a hospital.

Hard skin on the soles. Early every morning walk out barefoot in the dewy grass until your feet are thoroughly soaked in the dew. Wipe the feet dry and put a rag soaked in warm linseed oil over the hard skin at the bottom of your feet and bandage your feet up—if possible for the rest of the day. After two or three days of this treatment you will be able to scrape off the unwanted skin very easily. Soaking the feet in water is not as good as walking on the morning dew as there is something in the grass that helps in the softening-up process.

Horses. Treating horses was men's work. In our tribe it was usually done by my father.

A broken-winded horse must never be stabled. It must be kept out of doors in all weathers. In the summer months it is a good idea to swim a broken-winded horse in the river. A broken wind cannot be cured in a horse. In the case of a mare the symptoms can be reduced to the point where the mare is to all intents and purposes cured for some time—but the trouble will return and treatment will have to be repeated.

One remedy is a mixture of wood-tar and anis-seed. The other, more potent, remedy takes time to prepare and knowledge to use. You take the entrails of a freshly killed chicken, preferably a young cockerel, and seal them in a bottle, which you bury in a warm midden for two or three weeks; in this short period they will decompose out of contact with the air and produce an oil that can be drained off, and used as the most effective treatment for broken wind in a mare. I will not describe the way you administer the remedies—they might well kill a man who tried to use them on himself for a similar complaint.

The wood-tar and anis-seed remedy is also used for asthma in horses. There are a number of other remedies for asthmatic horses, including a ball made up of wood-tar, anis-seed and treacle; lard and saltpetre; a pinch of tobacco soaked in half a pint of water; a piece of twist—a piece of shag.

Another complaint in horses is a setfast. This is caused by the harness seesawing over a particular spot. We used to take them off, and to stop them bleeding we used to use caustic soda.

A setfast is like a big boil. It has a root like a parsnip which goes right deep into the horse, and if it is not removed it will heal up inside the flesh and keep growing into the body of the horse. To remove it we took a long carpet needle with a big eye, threaded in a length of bast-string,—that was the sort of string they tied bundles of hay up with—and after bathing the setfast until it was soft we drew the length of string through the head of the setfast with the carpet needle. We then threadled another length of bast-string into the carpet needle and drew that through the head of the setfast to form a cross inside the setfast, leaving the four ends dangling outside. Sometimes we just took the same string through again so that it formed a cross. The needle was, of course, removed.

The string cross was left in the setfast all night, so that fess went into that string. The next morning the string is pulled out and all the fess comes out with it. You bathe the setfast and then you are able to see the core. Once you could see the core you could get hold of it and pull it out—it is like a long piece of string. When you have got the core out you can draw the setfast out with a pair of pincers. Cut the skin out top of the hide and draw out the setfast—it is like a parsnip when you bring it out. I have seen them come out four and five inches long as they had grown right into the horse's backbone. Well, if the core has been got out and you managed to draw that setfast out completely, it's all right—but if just a small part of the growth remains in the horse's body, the setfast will come up again.

One year when we had just come back to the yard, a man from a very old established Romany family came to see my father, as they had a horse that was very queer. Also—the owner of that horse was very queer. When they told me of the symptoms of the man and his horse, I knew that they were both suffering from the strangles. So I told my father about these cases of the strangles as soon as he got home, and he agreed with me that these were definitely strangles cases.

He sent me down to the nearest woodworks—the nearest timber mill—to get a bag full of pitch pine sawdust. But the mill had no pitch pine sawdust, so I got some ordinary pine sawdust instead. As soon as I had brought back the bag of sawdust, my father and my grandmother got on the trolley and I drove them over to where the man and his horse were staying. My grandmother went to the wagon to see the man who had caught the strangles off the horse and my father went to see the horse. Some people call the strangles 'black-tongue'—but it has always been the strangles to us. The complaint starts off with an abscess at the back of the horse's throat, and through this abscess the horse keeps roaring; its nose runs and its eyes run, and the horse has got a temperature.

On our way over to this place my father bought a large bottle of pine disinfectant. When we got to doctoring the horse he told me to get a fire going—a nice big fire—and get the kettle boiling on the ground. My father cut a hole in each side of the bag of sawdust and tied a piece of string on, and tied the bag over the horse's head so that the horse's nose went into the bag of sawdust. When he had fitted the bag properly he removed it again and poured all the pine disinfectant into the sawdust. As soon as the kettle was a-boiling, he poured the boiling water onto the pine disinfectant and sawdust, and while it was a-steaming hot, he put the bag back onto the horse's head so that the horse breathed in the pine disinfectant—this is an inhalant that will gradually cure the strangles in a horse. If we had had pure pitch pine sawdust in the first place we would have had no need to use the pine disinfectant. The disinfectant is a very good substitute for the real thing, but it is not quite as good as the natural product.

Another thing in horses is called the spavin. There are several kinds of spavin. The type I am going to talk about is called a bone-spavin. A gentleman I was working for some years ago had bought a horse to go in his riding stable, and this horse had a lump on the outside of his left leg, right up into the second thigh. The gentleman asked me if this was an abscess and I told him that it wasn't. The lump had the scar of an operation on it. But whoever did the operation had botched the job. So, I told the gentleman that his horse had a bone-spavin, and if it were not operated on properly it would keep on coming. I explained to him how such a spavin was caused. At some time or other this horse had been kicked by another horse and the bone was splintered from the thigh. But it was not a complete break—one end of the splinter was still intact on the thigh bone. So the piece of splinter was still a living part of the thigh, and the nerves were still alive. This now made a separate bone with a new growing point—like the twig of a tree with a bud on it—and it kept on growing. Such a spavin will keep on growing through the flesh, and if it is not doctored it will continue growing outwards outside the horse's flesh.

Now this bone had been cut off, but it had not been cut off close enough to the second thigh. To do this you have got to open up the horse's leg, take the flesh at each side of the incision with a pair of forceps, stop the bleeding, and then plane off the bone right close to the thigh bone—as close as you possibly can,—and after you have taken the bone off, you have to stop the thigh bone from bleeding with a certain herbal liquid, and then you stitch the wound up with gut string. My father never had a recurrence of a bone-spavin, and I recommended him to the gentleman, but he did not want my father to treat his horse—he called in the local vet and it cost him a lot of money, about ten times what my father would have charged him!

Lost cures. When my grandmother was a girl, some of the women used to put certain types of mouldering cultures on cotton rags and bandaged the mouldy side over infected wounds. This reduced the infection and eventually healed the wound in the same way as raw honey. In this older school of Romany medicine they also sometimes used a particular extract from one of the poisonous toadstools, which they smeared around the uninfected area around a badly infected wound. The smell of this extract attracted a particular breed of fly that was allowed to settle on the infected wound. This fly completely cleaned up the infection by eating it away. Once the infection was gone, the fly completely lost interest in the wound and flew away. At this point raw honey was slapped onto the wound and it was bandaged up and left to heal. Unfortunately nobody seems to be around today who remembers how the mouldy cultures and the toadstool extracts were prepared—or which type of fly does not spread an infection but cures infections instead. The trouble is that since all this knowledge was passed on by word of mouth and a lot of the adepts would take their secrets to the grave rather than pass them on, a lot of useful knowledge had always been lost and may never be rediscovered again.

The end of the tradition. Nowadays most Gypsies go to the chemists for their medicines. You can no longer be sure that the old cures will help any more. The plants we used to use for medicines might be poisoned by insecticides and other sprays, artificial manures, exhausts from cars and any of the hundreds of other modern poisons that are transported by road. The old diet has also become less common. A lot of Gypsies today live out of tins, tinned fish, meat and so on—mouse-trap cheese, pickles, bread and dripping, fish & chips; and so they are not as well as they used to be before the war.

Nowadays most Gypsies and travellers are crammed together on dirty, dusty encampments with poor facilities where it is difficult to keep clean and keep up Romany standards. Snotty-nosed kids, caked with dirt, play with scrap and bring the mud and grease into the wagons. The women have the devil's own job trying to keep their places clean. There is no regular work available for most of the men. Worst of all, most of the women no longer seem to know how to cope with even the simplest ailments. As a result of all this, every case of anything at all in an encampment turns into an epidemic, and all the patients have to go into the care of local G.P.s and hospitals. Some people would call this 'progress'—I would say that it is a case of decline. To me it is a great tragedy that there are so few Romanies about and so many Didikais, pikies and scrap-dealers. They are all enterprising people; some of them, particularly the Scots travellers, are even very nice people, but they are a mere shadow of the old Roms.

7   The Mulo

In the old days before most of the Romanies became Christians they all believed in mulos, which were Romany dead men before they finally were allowed to the land of the dead. How long they haunted their particular part of the country depended entirely on how wicked they were in their lives. A good Rom that died was never supposed to become a mulo at all but went straight to the land of the shadows. The mulo was supposed to live inside the body of a dead man lying in his grave, but he came out of the tomb every night as the dead man's double and at cock-crow he returned to his grave until high noon when he came out for half an hour. If you got in his path you would have a terrible vengeance on your head—you would commit suicide or commit some terrible crime or if you were a woman, the mulo would rape you and you would give birth to an idiot child. Some said that the mulo was not a dead man at all but the devil in the guise of a dead man. But whichever way they looked at the mulo they were afraid of him and made a point of stopping at a camping site in time to get out of the mulo's way inside their tents or wagons. So the old Gypsies years ago never travelled at noon and were out of sight by dusk. Whenever a tribe took to religion—that is, when they became Christians—they dropped most of their older beliefs, and anybody who kept on worrying about mulos was in great danger of being turned out of the tribe. So it turns out that most of the pure Romanies in this country no longer bother about the mulos and travel at any time of the day or at night if they have to, while a good many of the Didikais and Pikies are still very particular about keeping out of the mulos's way. In our family the belief in the mulos was a very useful weapon for clearing an area more or less permanently of Pikies. One of the first tricks of this nature occurred well before my time—well before the general use of the motor car in fact. I am not sure about the exact area or even the approximate date when this occurred—but it is a true story as I got it from one of my uncles and it filled the newspapers at the time and caused a great sensation. As far as I can recall, it happened in the county of Somerset.

That night, as everybody in the area found first thing in the morning, the devil walked right across the county of Somerset. Only it wasn't the devil at all but some seven Romany tribes using over 400 sets of measure-stilts with size twenty-seven boots at their base. The whole operation took over eighteen months to plan out and prepare, and the reason for it was that on a particular stretch that had always been a Romany drom as far back as anyone could remember a lot of Pikies had drifted in and caused a lot of trouble for the Romanies. Now I don't know exactly how a measure-stilt was constructed, but I do know that it consisted of a pair of step-ladders that could be lengthened or shortened by means of slides and hinges. They were joined on top by a wheel. The bottom of each step-ladder stood in the great big boot and the man operating the stilts stood on one of the ladders and joggled about on it to make as deep a foot impression as possible. Then he would either swing the second ladder over the top by the wheel—if there was enough head room—or, if there was not enough room, he would raise the ladder by the slide and move it forward by one 'devil's stride'. Either way he got an exact measure of a stride, as the measure-stilts were constructed so that they could not over- or under-stride the three yards it was meant to do.

When the second ladder had been shifted to the front, the 'stilt-treader' stepped onto it and shifted the first ladder in front of it again. Then he joggled about on the second ladder to make a deep impression and stepped forward onto the first ladder again—and so he went on without ever stepping off the measure-stilts for the whole operation. This was straightforward enough while striding over open country, except that is was done on a dark night and required skilful balancing all the way—but going over hedges, ditches and country lanes posed a serious problem as people might be using the highways and lanes and see a man working the measure-stilts. So when he worked his way over and along a public right of way he had to throw a sheet over the whole works so that the devil would be seen walking rather than a man with ladders on boots. Walking with that cloak over the top he saw even less of what he was doing than when he walked over the fields.

The devil was supposed to walk right across Somerset in as straight a line as possible—he was not supposed to make any detour around houses or churches or barns and so on, but his footsteps had to go straight up one wall, over the roof and down the other wall. The stilt-treader could not walk up walls—he had to straighten out his stilts to turn them into a long ladder and then make a muddy line of 'devil's strides' with a spare set of twenty-seven size boot-seal-impressions; halfway over the top he had to hoist the ladder up and swing it the right way round and without too much noise over to the other side of the building. This was the snaggiest part of the whole business as it required exceptional physical strength and poise. Also, dogs were bound to bark in some of the farm buildings that were being boot-marked and if any of them brought a farmer out of bed the cat would have been out of the bag.

If any man tried to play this trick on his own he would do well if he managed to cover two miles in one night. It would be quite a feat if he managed to cross two cottages or one village church—but that night the devil walked the breadth of Somerset, because there were seven Romany tribes in this and between them they used well over 400 measure-stilts. The route of it was planned very carefully and every part of it studied over a period of about eighteen months. When the plan was put into operation it went off without a single hitch. After the men got back with their measure-stilts a party made their way over to the devil's trail from each of the camping sites and busied themselves with obliterating the tracks made to and from the devil's-strides by the 'stilt-treaders'. The next day the devil's footprints could be seen clearly along the whole route. It put the fear of God into all the locals—but that was not the point of the exercise. For the next few years it kept the area free from Pikies and Didikais who swore blind it was a mulo that had crossed and they were not going to take any chances.

Near to our yard, where we used to spend the winter months, there was a particular paddock that was used by Romanies as far back as anyone could remember and nobody ever seemed to have any objection to that in the past; but one year a lot of Didikais and Pikies pulled onto a part of it. It was well away from where the Romanies used to pull on but that made no difference—we knew for sure that that would mean a lot of trouble for us in the future if we did not get rid of them pretty smartly. Almost as soon as these people were on this paddock people in the neighbourhood started to loose their rabbits and chickens. Well, we knew who was responsible and we said so—but we all were getting the blame for it. So we decided to do something about it. We just had to get these people to leave and never to come back into this particular area. This was another case where the old mulo came in very handy—but this time I played a major part in working the spell and so it is a bit easier to talk about it. Some of my uncles went down to the pub on this particular evening and started to talk about the old mulo that sometimes comes round to haunt the particular plot where they were a-camping, telling them things like, 'I wouldnt' atch in that tan, if I was you, mush, the ole muller'll be arter you'— and things like that; they had some real good stories for them— but, of course that lot just laughed at that stage. Then my uncle came up to me and said, 'I'll show you what to do', and he dressed me up with a sheet with a big rubber band round the head and with two torches held by the rubber band under the sheet and shining through the sheet. They painted me with luminous paint. When it was getting dark I got onto my bike—it was one of those oldfashioned twenty-eight inch wheel uprights and I rode over to this Pikie encampment just as the people were getting into their tents for the night. Of course there were a lot of tents there at the time—but I headed straight towards a particular tent which I knew was not pitched too well and would collapse as soon as I hit it. I rode straight into this tent, praying that neither of my wheels would become entangled in the canvas and have me over as that would have been the end of me—but I was lucky and had the tent down and rode right over the top of it —in fact I could feel a bump as I rode over the legs of the bloke inside. You should have heard them scream! I never heard such a hullaballoo in my life. The bloke and the woman crawled out of their collapsed tent and they screamed and screamed the place down, and of course all the other Pikies came out of their tents and for the next few minutes all hell broke loose all over the encampment. I rode twice round this encampment and then straight up into an adjoining yard where I whipped off my sheet and things and put it in a bag. Then I wheeled the bike home by a detour. The next morning they were all gone from the paddock. As far as I know, no Pikie has ever been seen in that neighbourhood again. The legend of the old mulo in this area is still alive today. In those days in the local paper they reported that there was a man with glaring eyes—he was supposed to frighten women in the area and had caused miscarriages. Well, the travellers who fled from this paddock said that they had seen the man with the glaring eyes and that he was very tall and luminous and moved about with great speed; and, of course, all our family from this day forth all insisted that they had seen the man with the glaring eyes as well, and so nobody ever got to the bottom of this.

A lot of the travellers are very superstitious; they'd see something and mistake it for something else. Then they imagine things that could not possibly ever happen and talk about these things until they really believe that they'd seen things that don't exist. Then they make their people—their sons and daughters—believe that they had seen something that doesn't exist. And their sons and daughters will pass it on to their sons and daughters that this thing did exist and in due course these things seem to become almost a part of their religion.

Where we used to live there was a gravel pit and the gravel was pumped out by a steam-engine. When they used to pump this gravel, the water on the top of the pit used to form a whirlpool and you could hear that suck all the time they operated the pump. The Romanies around there used to call this the whirly-hole. There was a footpath that ran up alongside of this gravel pit and at the end of this footpath was a style that went over the railway. On the other side of the style was a big estate that belonged to Lord George Hatfield. On the particular night that I am going to tell you about now—it was dusk, it was half light—and a couple of chaps and myself were inside the fence in Lord George Hatfield's estate poaching. Well, I looked over the fence to see if there was a keeper coming when I saw an old Romany whom we used to call uncle Sam—Sam Smith, his name was. And he was coming up this footpath as fast as he could go, looking out behind him as he went and obviously trying to get back to his wagon before nightfall. So I said to the lads, I said, 'Come on, we'll have a bit of fun.'

Each side of the style was iron-spiked railings and it was a corrugated fence just there. I picked up a stick and as Sam got level with me to get over the style I ran the stick along the corrugated iron fence. RRRRRRRRRRRRR!!!!! it went. Hupp!—he didn't get over the style—he jumped over the style like a deer and in his jumping the iron spiked railing got caught in the back of his coat so he nearly went flat on his face in the mud—but he managed to get back his balance and, instead of stopping to lift his coat off the railing, in his fright he tore his coat—he wrenched it off—and he was over the next style on the other side of the footpath and away like a greyhound. I never seen an old one move that fast in my life!—and the next day when we saw him he swore blind that he had seen the devil. He said the devil appeared to him and sithered his coat down by the whirly-hole; and he swore to that till the day he died—and his sons to this day still swear blind that their father had seen the devil.

The sort of tricks that I am talking about here worked only if your victims believed that a place was visited by a mulo or the devil himself. If you missed the right time for haunting a place to rid it of Pikies, you could forget about that place as a camping ground from then on. For instance, there was a particular place in Kent, a disused chalk pit where my father stopped a lot throughout his life and so did his father and grandfather on the few occasions they were in this part of the country. We used to stop there once or twice in every year. There was a five-part gate across the front. We used to pull in with our wagons. The woman in the corner-shop allowed us to go round the back of her shop for water. We had built a corral at one end to put our horses on at a small charge, and we used to stop there for about a week at a time. We did this for years. Nobody ever interfered with us at all. We still stopped there for a bit after the war. One day, soon after we had left the place, some Pikies pulled in there. They smashed the front gate; they pulled down the corral; their horses were running wild, getting into people's gardens trampling everything under; they threatened the woman in the shop and smashed up a local pub; they cut down some trees for firewood and they did their business all over the place. Of course, after a time the police stepped in and the local authorities had these Pikies shifted—and that put the kybosh on that. Nobody was ever allowed to stop there again in a tent or a wagon. Now, if we had handled that lot, the old mulo might have shifted those Pikies before things had got out of hand.

8   Marriage

Years ago the marriage customs were very, very strong. If you were a Romany travelling in the tribe, you were supposed to marry into the Romany race; if you married out of the Romany race without the consent of your chief you were discarded—you were pushed aside; and it was not very often that a non-Romany marriage partner was acceptable to the chief of the tribe. In many tribes it was also the custom for the parents to choose your partner for you. But today this sort of thing is very rare indeed. If a young Romany picks up with a girl who happens to be a Gorgio, and he takes her home to see the head of the tribe and the head takes a liking to that girl, the chap can marry her and remain a member of the tribe. But if the chief takes a dislike to her and tells the chap, 'No, you won't marry her', but the chap says to himself, 'I ain't taking no notice of the old buzzard!', and he marries her anyway, well, then he is thrown out of the tribe for keeps. It would be no use for him to change his mind after a few months and say he is sorry and that he'll be a good boy if they'll take him back after he has got his divorce—they'll never take him back. But there are many nowadays that have married Gorgio girls, and also Romany girls have married Gorgio husbands. But years ago it never used to take place at all except for reasons of strong breeding once in every four or five generations.

If a chap is in the hop field, or is in the fruit country and he sees a young girl he takes a fancy to—he looks at her and she looks at him—he'll either talk to her the first chance he gets or he'll give her his dicklo—that's the scarf he has around his neck. Now, when he sees that girl again and she is wearing his dicklo as a headscarf he knows that she will go out walking with him. Well, then they go out walking for a time and then they will decide on a day to go off together.

Well, they go off together—jump the broomstick, as they call it, and they live together for several days. They'll build a bender—that's a tent—he will buy a cooking pot; if he hasn't got a kharvie-saster—that's a kettle-iron—he will make one and they will live together for several days to see if they suit; and if they suit each other they'll come back to the tribe and are first married in the Romany tradition, or some part of the old ceremony anyway and there will be a great wedding feast. Then, a few days later there will be a church wedding in most cases but some will just register their marriage, while some others again still think that the Romany wedding is sufficient. If the couple find out in time that they are not for each other, the marriage is broken off right at the start; otherwise, of course, they'll be rowing and fighting and half killing one another. That's the way most of them go on today.

Many of the old Romany tribes used to marry into each other and some of the tribes to this day won't even consider marrying out of their own blood. Marriage between second and third cousins was not as common as marriage between first cousins, but there was practically no bar against marrying any relative within the tribe or with the same family name, except that you were not in any circumstances allowed to marry your father, mother or one of your children. Outside your own tribe you could only marry Romanies from certain allied or related tribes which were accepted as blood relations even though they might not have been related at all. For instance, the Boswells were always acceptable to the Woods—and so were the Ingrams. The Ingrams, incidentally, were the only Romany tribe travelling in England before the Wars of the Roses. There is a lot of talk about them being extinct, but there are still a few of that name in the country; Peter Ingram is one of them—very good craftsmen in wood, they are, and I am not ashamed to own that they are related to me through another line in the family. To come back to the marriage subject—if a Gypsy wanted to marry outside his own blood, and also outside of one of the allied or related tribes he had to get a special dispensation from the head of his tribe. With the Wood tribe there was a tendency to encourage an occasional mixed marriage with a Gorgio.

Now, for the correct old courting and marriage customs in the tribes as far as they are still remembered and partly observed. If a man wishes to marry a particular girl, he gives her his neckerchief; if she puts it on as a headscarf, they are engaged; if she does not, there will be no wedding. If the girl has accepted the scarf and wears it, the man goes to her father and asks him for the hand of his daughter in marriage, and the father turns him down flat. Then the couple elope for a while and live together somewhere where nobody is likely to find them. This is sometimes difficult. Eventually they come back to the tribe—if they are from two different tribes, they come back to her tribe, and after a bit of a scene the girl's family arranges for a wedding. They invite a lot of guests—mainly members of the tribe—to a wedding. But they will never mention whose wedding they are inviting them to.

There are two ceremonies used for marriage that I know of: jumping the broomstick and mingling of blood. The broomstick ceremony is the shorter of the two and it is used less than the blood-mingling ceremony. All that you do for this is for the couple to hold hands while they jump over a besom made of flowering thorn or gorse in front of members of their families. I have often heard of people having broomstick weddings but I don't know of any Romany today who actually used such a ceremony when he got married. But in the last century I know for a fact that some of the Welsh Gypsies did get married in that way. All the ones I know went in for the mingling of the blood.

According to one of the old stories about a king of the Gypsies there was a marriage ceremony lasting two and a half hours where one of the elders of the tribe recited a long sermon while the couple sat side by side facing him. The groom occasionally had to give set answers to some of the questions the elder asked him in between the sermon, and during a number of sentences in the sermon the elder threw flower petals at the bride and groom. After this rather long initial ceremony the bride and groom had to jump over a besom of broom, a toolbox, and a musical instrument and a set of fortune-telling cards. Then the couple stood up facing the elder—man to the right, his bride to the left, holding hands. The next part of the ceremony is the bit most of the Romanies use at the present time when they get married. Instead of an elder it is now usually the groom's father conducting the blood-mingling ceremony—but sometimes it is the bride's father. The elder had a young unmarried girl standing at either side of him—the one to his right had a silk cord and a pointed knife in her hands. The other girl held a bunch of twigs. These twigs came off seven different kinds of trees; there was a magic recitation as the elder snapped them one by one and threw them to the winds. Then he told the couple of the meaning of the marriage bond and that it was wrong to break their pledge to one another until either of them had died; he told them that they would have to give and share. Then he told the bride to go and fetch the bread, the salt and the water. She went over to her tent, took a basket with a loaf of bread and a small bag of coarse sea salt in it and also a small bucket which she filled in the stream.

She came back to her man and the elder; the groom took a small cup out of his pocket and filled it from the bucket. They both drank from the cup which they then smashed —and this was the only time ever that they were allowed to use the same cup in their lives—and he had to drink first. Then came the mingling of the blood. The man held out his right hand and his bride held out her left hand. The elder squeezed their wrists and pierced them so that they would bleed slightly. He then put their wrists together, so that their blood would mingle, and he wrapped the silk cord round and made three knots into the cord —one for constancy, the next for fertility and the last for long life. The elder unwrapped the cord and broke the small loaf of bread in half. He squeezed the wound on the bride's wrist until he got some of her blood onto one half of the loaf which he gave to the groom; he squeezed the wound on the groom's wrist until he got some of his blood on the other half of the loaf which he gave to the bride. The couple then had to eat the bread with the blood. When every bit of blood on the bread had gone, the rest of the loaf was broken over the couple's heads.

Then they took the bag of salt and took some of its contents out and threw it over their left shoulders. The elder then gave them half each of the silk cord with the blood on it that had been round their wrists. These half silk cords they had to keep for two years—just in case they wanted to part company again within that period. They could only be parted again by that same elder within that period—and if that elder died before they decided to split up, then they could never be parted again at all. But within that two-year period the elder could put them through a divorce ceremony in front of witnesses in which he would burn the two half cords to end the marriage. Then—coming back to the old marriage ceremony—the elder gave them a kharvie-saster, which is a kettle-iron, to drive away evil spirits. And that was the end of that long ceremony. The small bucket the bride had fetched the water in earlier on was placed on the camp fire and now the couple leap over this boiling kettle on the fire and take their leave from the gathering. Some of the wedding guests busy themselves with flattening the bucket with a sledge hammer. The couple leave at once and the wedding guests eat and drink too much and have a roaring good time.

The Gypsy wedding ceremony nowadays does not last two and a half hours. If it takes more than ten minutes everybody gets restless; it if takes only two minutes nobody is either surprised or upset. I very much doubt if there is a Romany in the whole world who remembers all of the ancient wedding ceremony—but there must be lots who still know the prince's wedding story—even in the old Romany language. What has happened is that each Romany tribe just took over one or the other part of the ceremony and carried it on as their own. Most of them go in for the mingling of the blood only; some just hold hands before witnesses of their tribes; and others still might jump over the broomstick—though I have yet to meet someone who got married in this way. Whichever ceremony they go through, you can bet your life on it that they will refer to their wedding as a 'broomstick wedding'. And within weeks most of them will nowadays get themselves married for a second time in a church or a registry office.

9   Death

Years ago when one of our people died they put him in a caravan with all of his possessions and set the lot alight. According to one of the old stories, if it was one of the chief men in a tribe, his wife would go into the wagon with him before it was set alight to be burned with him. But that was many centuries ago. In those days no Romany ever lived in a wagon, but he had a flat trolley that was drawn by a donkey or mule when he travelled, and on it he carried all of his possessions—clothes, tools, furniture and so on. He sometimes rode on horseback, but more often he walked leading the donkey or mule, and his wife or wives and children walked behind the trolley looking straight ahead. Such a trolley was sometimes covered with a bender tent— a bit like a canvas-topped wagon of today. Whenever they stopped off somewhere they pitched tents and took everything off the trolleys. They slept in the tents. The trolleys or primitive wagons were only here for transporting them from place to place.— When any one died one of those wagons or trolleys was used for a funeral pyre. Most of the dead person's possessions were burned at the same time.

But nowadays most of the people on the road are buried like anybody else. A few are cremated and the ashes thrown to the winds in one of their favourite localities, but most of them are buried in a churchyard. Years ago they used to burn the lot—body, wagon, all their clothes and so on, and whatever wouldn't burn, like their china ware, would be smashed; and what couldn't be smashed up or burned would be knocked out of shape with a sledge hammer. The dead person's dogs would be shot; and the horses and other animals; and whatever couldn't be destroyed was supposed to be buried or thrown in a deep pond or river. Nothing whatsoever could be sold. Women were always to be buried or burned with all of their jewellery except one ring which could be left to their eldest daughter. This ring sometimes remained in the line of the eldest daughter for centuries. Only money was not normally either destroyed or buried. Today mostly only the wagon is burned and the cups, bowls and plates smashed up and the cutlery made useless. Everything else is distributed. With all these expensive trailers coming into vogue I shouldn't wonder if a lot of them won't burn their caravans in the future.

There are all sorts of other things I could tell about on the subject of death and burial. There's parts of Hampshire that I could take you to and I could show you flints there laid in the side of the road where Gypsies had been cremated and had their ashes scattered. Any time a tribe passes one of their flint crosses they repair them. Sometimes they burned a body and kept the ashes until they reached a particular part of the county some good distance from where the body had been cremated and then scattered the ashes. Sometimes they went to a crossroads, sometimes to a sharp bend in the road, or sometimes to the spot where the person was known to have been born at the side of the road. But, of course, that is all changed now. They still bury things—sometimes with the body in the coffin; if, for instance, a man was a good fiddler, they would not burn or smash up his fiddle when he died, but they would put it undamaged into his coffin with him. That is why his coffin would be made extra big if his people had someting like this in mind. Also, at the place where he had died, and at various other places which had some important part in his life they might bury an old axehead or an old billhook, or an old saw. It's still done by some of them to this day—an old pot or a kharvie-saster or anything like that, they'd bury at the side of the road or in a wood, or in a copse or wherever they think they can best bury the evil spirits that have been released when the person died. That was the whole point of burying these things. In fact, when they buried a kharvie-saster—they knocked it right into the ground as deep as they possibly could ram it, because that pegged the evil spirits right deep into the bosom of the earth—or so they thought.

Before the burial or cremation of a body, it was the usual custom to lay it out to view in an open coffin. In the past most of the jewellery and some money of the dead person was put into the coffin, though sometimes these things were buried separately. As long as the body lay unburied and even after the end of the funeral—until at least an hour after they were back on the road after the funeral—none of the grown-ups were allowed to eat or drink anything except dry bread and water. Children were not expected to fast; but they were encouraged to do so. They were not allowed to eat meat either, mainly because there was a definite bar against cooking during the wake.

While the body was lying on view it was continually watched over. There were always supposed to be three kins-women staying with a body for the whole time it was laid out to view. All three had to keep awake from start to finish of the wake. Apart from these three, members of the dead person's family had to spend a certain amount of time with the corpse. There were generally two candles kept burning—one at the head and one at the feet of the corpse—but sometimes there was only one burning at the head end of the coffin. The handling and laying out of the corpse was always supposed to be done by people outside of the tribe, and if possible, not by Gypsies but by Gorgios. A dying person was supposed to dress impeccably in his or her best clothes and shoes and lie down to die on top of a carpet laid on the deathbed. Sometimes this was made ready in a death tent. All this, of course was only possible when the person sensed the approach of death within the hour.

The undertakers were never supposed to measure the body, but bring a coffin that was certainly too large. They were not to handle the corpse but they had to lift it into the coffin by the carpet and then manoeuver it into position. The coffin had to hold the fully clad corpse, with jewellery, perhaps a fiddle, hammered dulcimer or a tambourine, as well as some favourite items of the deceased—such as his pipe, his silver or pewter tankard, his whip, deer-skinner's knife, walking-stick or his gun. Most of them had at least some money buried with them, some of them a lot—even new gold coins if the person was important enough in the tribe. In the case of a woman, this money would be either dropped into her apron before the coffin was shut, or else placed in pockets in a broad ornamental belt round her waist.

Nowadays fewer things get buried with the corpse and most people are not wearing shoes when they get buried. They are more concerned with dying in comfort than they used to be and it would be very difficult to put shoes on a person who is already dead.

10   Conclusion

There is a lot of talk by the settled people about the Romanies trying not to change with the times, a lot of talk about us being irresponsible and not being able to adjust to the present over-crowded and mechanized conditions. It is also thought that our people have an unrestricted freedom that cannot be tolerated by a civilized society, but must be fettered. I believe that I have shown in my book that all these impressions are pure fancy. Our people were always a good deal less free than the settled people we came in contact with. Only we felt more free because our way of life was nearer to nature and therefore closer to our natural instincts. In fact we have changed a good deal more than the house-dwellers over the past few centuries, and particularly since the Second World War when the old system of the tribe, with the common purse and all the rest of it, had practically ceased to exist.

In the old way the only time a Romany was free was when he was alone; but even then he was not really free because he was doing something he had been ordered to do by the head of his family. He had a certain amount of choice as to when he would get up in the morning and when he would turn in at night. He would also sometimes have a certain amount of choice as to the exact order in which he would do his assigned jobs; but he had no choice at all as to the quality of the work, and he was obliged to finish it by a given time. The man was always the boss, and his womenfolk were virtually his slaves. In the beginning of the last century he still had the power of life and death over his women. If he discovered that any of them broke any one of the old Romany codes he could kill or maim her—maybe slash off one of her ears or split her nose with a knife; or if he found that his wife—or one of his wives—had been unfaithful to him he could have her buried alive by his kinsmen.

A woman could never be the equal of a man or become his boss unless she was declared fit to sit in Council after she was past the child-bearing age. Once she was accepted in this way as an elder she could, if she was thought superior, become the chief of the tribe. But before she could reach such a position she had to spend more than forty years as a bonded servant of the tribe. All her earnings, and all the earnings of her children up to the age of about seventeen went into the common purse held by the chief of the tribe. She was in charge of her sons only as long as she could control them; after that dad took them over. The men only had to give a certain fraction of their earnings to the tribe, but the women and children had to give it all.

The women had a certain number of rights which they could insist on just as long as they accepted every restriction that was put on them by the Romany code. Since the breaking up of most of the old tribes, particularly after the Second World War, and after the increased influence of the Gypsy evangelists, family life has become more relaxed and happier on the road. Quite a lot of Gypsies still beat their wives regularly, but the majority have come round to thinking that it is not right to rough-handle a woman. There is also a certain risk in it nowadays. In the old days the women took what was coming to them, but nowadays, often as not, they fight back, and some of them give as good as they get. I know of one particular case—I won't mention any names—but it is a Romany in Kent, and he decided that his wife was due for a good hiding, and she gave better than she got; in fact he got the biggest tanning of his life, and since then she is the boss. Even thirty years ago I doubt if she would have got away with it because his kinsmen would have worked her over; but nowadays they just have a good laugh at his expense and reckon it serves him right. Besides, thirty years ago I doubt if any woman could have resisted her husband if she had tried. The men were all trained as fighters from a very early age, as there were many occasions in their lives when they had to take care of themslves. The women only learned a few tricks in case they were molested by any of the locals, but this didn't happen very often, because the Romanies had a reputation for evening up old scores.

I have been asked many times would I like to live in a house. This is something I just can't explain to people and to make people understand, as living in a house is not my idea of life at all. I have lived in caravans—horse-drawn and trailer—all of my life. I am a man of the wilds, of the open air, of the fields and the woods, and I could not be this if I lived in a house. When I live in a caravan I can sometimes see the branches of a tall tree through the skylight, and it is not always the same tree, and I can hear all the sounds of nature clearly—like in the open—when I lie abed at night; the sounds of nature that I would only hear in the distance and muffled if I lived in a house. When I step out of my caravan I like to feel the green grass under my feet; and I like to see the birds flitting in and out of the hedgerows; and after a day's work I like to have a good wash and sit beside my fire on the ground to have a meal of natural food—this wish is nowadays not always fulfilled—and to have a drink of tea with the smell of the wood fire in it. I like to listen to the last song of the blackbird in the evening, and as it begins to get dark I like to watch the stars come out and the moon come up—all in their natural full glitter. I like to listen to the song of the nightingale and the hooting of the owls and the screeches of the bat as he rushes through the air catching insects. I like the beating of the rain on the roof of the wagon and the singing of the wind through the treetops—the feeling of relief when you come to a stopping place and out of the gloom and the doom of a bad spell. I like to listen to the grunt of the badger in the undergrowth and the clicking of a cricket in the thicket; and at the right time of the year I like to hear the cry of the vixen and the dog fox. I like to listen to the buzzing of the bees as they fly from bloom to bloom along a hedgerow and I like to see the colours on the wings of the butterflies. I even like the constant change from extreme comfort to extreme discomfort that is an essential part of living a good healthy life, and I like the feeling of uncertainty, of never knowing quite what lies around the corner though I might know the area well, and I like the feeling that, come what may, I will be able to win through in all circumstances as long as I rely on myself and remain a Romany. These are the things that make up my life; I would like to have all of them and many more that I have not mentioned, all in their season all of the time—and I could only have the smallest fraction of them if I settled down in a house.

Beyond that,

> You can trust a Romany for your best friend
> You can trust a Romany to the end;
> He won't rob you, he won't lie—
> You can trust him till you die;
> But, hate him, and you'll come off worse,
> For he can haunt you with a curse!

The Speech of the
English Romanies

Nowadays no English Romany that I know of can still speak or even understand the old Romany language that I described earlier on in the book. The last three Welsh Romanies to speak the language perfectly without mixing any English or Welsh into it were Manfri, Howell and Jim Wood of Bala, Merioneth. They are all dead now. There are still a number of quite good Welsh Romany speakers around even today, but they all mix a certain amount of English and Welsh into their Romany, and their grammar is not as pure any more as that of the three people I have mentioned. To get an idea of what Romany was like at the time when it was still a language in its own right in this country, one has to study John Sampson's book, *The Dialect of the Gypsies of Wales;* and to get an idea of the right intonation of the language one can listen to a recording of a Welsh Romany conversation between Manfri and Howell Wood at Bala—recorded by Peter Kennedy, and available for students at the Sound Library, Cecil Sharp House, Regent's Park Road, London NW1.

The Romany spoken by English Gypsies today is best described as an English dialect that contains a certain amount of Romany, slang and old cant. It is not often that any of us actually speak in this dialect. We only slip into it when we hold a confidential conversation of the type a Gorgio would have between his own four walls. In a sense we are always in the public eye, and even when one is not particularly trying to hide anything it is good to be able to have some private conversation whenever one feels the need to. Nowadays, I doubt if any English Gypsy uses more than about 150 Romany words in the course of one years' conversation—I use rather fewer than 150 myself nowa-

days, though I can understand probably 2,000 Romany words if I hear them. Before the war my grandparents still spoke whole sentences in the old Romany language in between English Romany speech, and they had Romany terms for every fruit, herb, flower, tree, bush and so on—hundreds of words that you would not even find in Sampson.

The word list I give here includes all the words I still use today and as many as I could recall of my grandparent's vocabulary. As to the pronunciation—this varies from speaker to speaker; 'u' and 'oo' in my spelling can be pronounced as either 'u' in 'but' or 'u' in 'put' or 'oo' in 'fool', 'a' in 'chavi' is like 'a' in 'hat', but it is a long vowel like the 'a' in 'far'. The English word 'far' is pronounced 'fur' in my part of the country; 'dog' is pronounced 'dogue'—to rhyme on 'rogue'—but it is a pure 'o' sound that does not lead into a 'u' as in standard English; also 'dogue' and a few other words would come out low as compared with the rest of the sentence, very similar to the drop of your voice when you sing 'never' in 'Auld Lang Syne'— 'and never brought to mind'. There are a number of other peculiarities in the pronunciation of some of the travellers when they switch over to the dialect; there is, for instance, the trick of not moving the lips when speaking it. If my father caught any of the youngsters in our tribe speaking like that he would whip them, as he considered this very bad manners, a debasement of the language and, what is worse, a Pikie trick.

So here, for what it is worth, is a list of all the words I could think of in the space of one week, with the best compromise spelling I could devise. To use these words, you would form English dialect sentences and weave them in where-ever they fit, for instance:

You're jessin to booti to yearn moro You are going to work to earn bread.
You're jessin to the buriker to fetch moro You are going to the shop to fetch bread.
You're jessing torarti to the kitchima You are going to the pub tonight.
The old rakli over akai's nafli; mandi dik'd the drabengro jessin to the

old rakli's kenner The old woman over here is ill; I saw the doctor going to her house.

Dick a'the rakli's yurr-drops! Mandi koms the rakli's yurr-dropps (or *year-drops*) Look at the woman's ear-rings! I like the woman's ear-rings.

Hush kacker Be quiet and listen.

Chin the bor Trim the hedge.

Lullered by the gavvers—to be taken by the police.

Pucker to the gero, chav, the old groi's too much vonger—Talk (bargain) to the man, mate, the old horse is too much money (is too dear).

The mush akai dicks like a pugurus The man here looks like a monkey.

A bori odjus tikner a big lovely baby.

Lel the kosh for the yog fetch the wood for the fire.

Oh, dick ai, chav, it's kowli te rati, it'll pan te rati Oh, look out, mate, it is dark tonight, it will rain tonight.

Vaster the togs akai Bring the clothes over here.

Mandi and tutooti let's jel akai—You and I, let us come (encamp) here.

Dick ai, chav, a mushkero jel Look out, mate, a policeman comes.

Put the Kavi oana saster Put the kettle on an iron (kettle-prop)

Mandi can year the bavel in the ruckers—I can hear the wind in the trees.

We'll be lelled We will be arrested.

Nash avri Go away.

Where you atchin? Where are you staying.

I have no explanation as to why certain words have remained in the language while others, describing things as common in everyday life, have disappeared. All I know is that when a word is no longer in general use on the road, the old speakers will stop using it too. One of the most puzzling things is the way the numerals have become more complicated since my grandparents' time. My father's parents and my father were the only Romanies I knew who could still, and did, use all the old Romany numbers up to tens of thousands. All the other speakers can only count up to five, and some of them remember the

Romany word for 'ten'—but quite a lot of them don't even remember the word for 'ten'. With all of them numbers six, seven, eight, nine, have gone the way of the raspberry and all the other dodos of the language; and with the majority ten and a hundred have also disappeared from the vocabulary. To say a simple number like 'seven'—which should be 'efta', you would nowadays have to recite a simple sum, for instance 'trin ta stor' or 'trin an stor' or 'duitrin ta yeck' or 'dui trins an yeck' or any other way you felt like at the time. But just for the record I have listed all the numerals my grandparents used in the word list. I hope that this, a fraction of what I had at my fingertips before the war, will be of use to any Gypsy scholar who happens to have got hold of this book.

Word List

adoi there
adrey, 'drey in into, within
akai here
av akai come here.
ambrol pear
arva, arvalie yes
atch, hatch to stay
atchava I stop, remain
atchen tan stopping place
av to come (*avel, 'vel, 'wel*)
avas let us come
avree away
jal avree go away
bak, bok Luck
bakalo lucky (*baktalo*, happy)
kushti bak, good luck
balovas bacon
bal, balum hair
bar a pound note
bárrikánni pheasant
bárripóari peacock
bang, beng the devil
baulo policeman
bauri snail
báuromátchi salmon
bavol, baval wind
becker fruit
beebi aunt

bender tent; noose on a spring
berk breast
bero ship
besh to sit; nest
bickin to sell
bister a summons
bístering mush judge, magistrate
bitcher to send, to transport
bítchado pardál sent across, transported
bitti little, small
bíttikánni partridge
bocklo hunger, hungry
si tut bocklo? are you hungry?
bokro sheep
boler wheel
boobi pea
booti work
bor friend; hedge
boreen a small country lane
bori, barri big
bosh violin
kel the bosh, play the fiddle;
boshoméngro, violinist, fiddler
(*balánokosht* is the violin bow)
broller pear
brembelia blackberry

122

brushíndo rain
bul bottom, behind
bun witch
bungy, bongo lame
búriker, buteker shop
busno billigoat
chad posterior
chai girl, young woman
chaipáni seagull
chal chap, fellow, man
char ashes
charo bowl, plate
chat, chet, chete a thing
chaunt to sing
chav term of endearment; child
'chav to stop (from atchav)
'chava I stop
'chavaia! stop!
chavi girl
chavo boy
cheuri knife
chib tongue, speech
chik dust, dirt
chíkchani frog
chikly dirty
chikni daughter
chikno son
chin to cut
chíngary a fight
chinner a hatchet
chiokers boots
chir to sing
chírilo, chíriko bird
chiténgro frog
chitries foliage, greens, herbs, vegetables
chiving putting
chókalis shoes

chockas boots
chooma kiss
chooper whip
chor to steal
chori poor
chover shop
choviar witch
chóvihánni witch
chuffa, chukka coat
chuffas petticoats
churi knife
coaver these
cóokerell pot
conger match
dacker toad
dadrus, dadus, dad father
púrodad grandfather
daia, dai, mother
púridaia grandmother
dal, del to give
dan to bite
dand tooth
danners teeth
deloméskro hammer
deram light
deriav sea, ocean
desh ten
déshshel thousand
Devel god
Develésko mush Jesus Christ
Didikai, Didikoi Gypsy outside the Romany tribes and of mixed blood
dik to look, see
dikkoméngro, dikkoglímmer mirror
dínilo's dikkaméngro a television set

diklo scarf
ding to throw
dinlo, dinilo, dinili silly, stupid; an idiot, a fool
divio, divi, didlo crazy
divvus day
djilia songs
dood light, moon
doosta enough, plenty
dordi, dordi the most common exclamation
drab poison
drabber chemist
drabéngro, drabméngro doctor
drabsap adder, viper (drábaneysapa)
drábaneysapa poisonous snakes
drag car (usually called a motor)
drom, drum road (plural: droma)
drummer rabbit
dui two
dukker, drukker to tell fortunes
dukkering, drúkkeribén fortune-telling
drúkkerébema a prophecy
dunnick cow
dur far
duro long
durrel berry
Duvvel God
dwin Three
dyker daffodil
eef snow
efta seven
emets ants

faida pegs
fake to make or mend
faster hand
fauni ring
feeter clothes-peg
filshinákos deer
foggus tobacco
fonga fork
foros fair, market
folki people
gad shirt
gájikano stranger
gatta, gadda beer
gav a town; to hide
gavver, gav mush policeman
Geyro, Geyri non-Gypsy man and woman
gilli song; (plural: gillia)
gilo gone, departed
giv corn
givéngro farmer
glaze, glazey, glazer window
goodlo sugar; sweet
góodlokénner beehive
gooi pudding
goolis testicles
goonna bag, sack
Gorgio, Gaujo non-Gypsy
grai horse
grannum corn
grasni mare
grauni gem
griddler bicycle
griga heather, ling
groi horse
groiéngero, Graiéngro horse-dealer
groovni cow (also gurni)

grov ox, bull (also *groovno* or *gurno*)

grunter pig

gry horse

gurli cherry

haréef ice

Haw to eat

Heréngro crab, lobster

hero leg; wheel of vehicle

hobben food

holéno landlord, publican

holofer sock, stocking

Hóokamen, hóckaben lie, fraud, deceit

Hotchi hedgehog

Hótchiméngri frying pan

hummel hair

Inneon nine

jarriger apron

jass run away

jaul to go (*jel* is used for to come)

jib language

jiffro coat

jigger door

jin to know, to understand

jinnik donkey

jívaben life

joob louse

joobly lousy

joovi woman

júckal, jook, jog, dogue dog

juvel, juvli women

kaba kettle

kackarátchi magpie

'kai, 'koi (akai) here

kair to make, to do

kako uncle

kal cheese

kam to love

kámmoben love, friendship

kang taste

kanni chicken, fowl

kanniechor chicken thief

kappar blanket

kari penis

kas hay

kassóni bill-hook

kauli black

káulochírilo blackbird

káulodúros bilberries; black-currants

kavvi, kharvi kettle

kávvisáster kettle iron

Kaydi hat

kek, kekka no, not

kekkávvi kettle

kennick house-dweller

kel to do, to play

kepsi basket

ker, ken, kenner house

keréngro house-dweller

ketter, ked to gather, to pick

ki to

kil butter

kin to buy

kipsi basket

kliss to shut

klissin lock

klíssiméngero trap

kókkero self

kokko uncle

kola things

kom love

konáfni turnip

konéngri hare

konyo peaceful, quiet
kooli soldier
kor to fight
kora a fight
kóraméngro boxer
koro cup
kosh, kosht wood, stick
kovva a thing
kraftni turnip
kuriying fighting
kushi, kusi a little
kushti good, fine, nice, all right
lacho good
lalo, lala red
lalos cherries
laster to find
lav, name word
lel to take, to catch
lévinor, livna, lívena beer
lévinorkénna pub, ale-house, inn (also called *kitchima*)
lévinorméngris hops
lil a book
lólochírillo redpole
lólodúianchír robin
lon salt
the bori lon pani 'the great salt water', the ocean
lóoverni prostitute
luller to arrest
mailo, moilo, myla donkey
mandi, man, me I, me; *mandi's,* my, mine
mas meat *maséngro,* butcher
matchi fish
matchko, matchiko cat
mato drunk

mélali smutty
meláno canary
meski tea
méripen death
miltog shirt
minj private part of female; vagina
misto well, all right
moaker mule
mókadi, mókado, móggerdowie ritually unclean; impure; dirty
mókadi jóok fox
mong to beg
monisha, monishi, mollisher wife, girlfriend; used to mean woman
monkri countryside
mooi face, mouth
móoikósht a whistle
moolyin matchi pike
moon month
sixmoon, six months
moosh man
morgan hare
morler hand
mort woman
morum, moro, panum bread
motto drunk
muk leave, let
mukka mule
múladi haunted by a dead person
mulésko dud will-o'-the-wisp
mulla, corpse
mulo, muladi, moolo ghost of Romany man or woman in possession of a corpse at

certain hours of the day and night; the devil in possession of a corpse

múlladipóov graveyard, cemetery

mumli candle

mumper, mumpli, hedgemumper, hedgecrawler tramp; traveller without any Romany blood

mumpli the ways of a mumper

mung to beg

muréngi berry

muréngimátchi trout

mush man

múshgaying to spy out the land

mushgro, musker policeman

nafli, násfalo ill

nantee, nanti don't

nappy obstinate (used mainly to describe a horse)

narked, narkri dark, dank, bad, unpleasant

nash to hang

nav name

nogo own

nok nose

nongo naked

odjus lovely, beautiful

ogrúsela gooseberry

oito eight

olivas stockings

opréy, 'prey up, upon

'*prey o poov*', on the ground, in the field

'*prey o pani*' on the river or lake

ora clock, watch, time

orélla trout

ozi heart

palésko nephew

panish hungry

pánishók watercress

pansh five

papin goose

pápingo gander

paramíkri rabbit-snare

patrin leaf

pattríensis herbs used in cures

páttrimíshi legend, story, fairy-tale

pauni, pani, parni water

pani, pan to rain

paurdál, pardál across

ped to walk

peeve, pee to drink

pen sister; to speak

penyáki niece

pester to pay

pero leg

petál hoof

petlar nut

Pikie Gypsy expelled from tribe

pir stomach

pirri foot

pishom bee

píshomgúdlo honey

pobble, pobo apple

pogger to beat; to break

poggered broken

pókinyos high-court judge

poodéllas bellows

pooker to ask, to tell

the kosht that pookers the drom, the pookering-kosh, signpost

póokersaméngri lawyer
póorami leek
póorano ancient
pooro, poori old
pootsi pocket
póover, poovéngro potato
posh half
poshes money
Poshrat halfbreed Gypsy
poshumésko woollen
povel apple
pral brother
praster to run
pug ferret; to hide
púgurus monkey
purchery fish pond, fish farm
puro old
purum onion
pushka gun (only used for a flintlock)
putch, putcha to ask, to enquire
pútcherléngro smith
Rai, rye gentleman
rakli girl
rákonis trousers
rap, rup silver
rashái priest, parson, minister
rarti night
rártigíllichal nightingale
rat blood
ratválo bloody, bleeding
rattlers beans
rauni lady
rokker to talk
Rom Romany man
rom, romer, bridegroom, husband

romered, ramado married
romni bride, wife
rómanichírilo water wagtail
rómanirétchka mallard
retchka a duck
retchko a drake
rosela, ribiséla redcurrant
rove, ruv to cry to weep
ruk, rukker tree
rúkkersaméngri squirrel
rull spoon
rummer to marry
rup, rupper silver
rúppavo chaffinch
rustler flower
sáliwésher bridle
sap, sarp, sapper snake
sappéskomátchi eel
saster iron; wire
sásterkábakósh kettle-iron
scran food
scroops hops
shant pint
shav, shab, sherp, shev to go
sharo, sherro head
shora, shura head person, foreman, gaffer.
shel hundred
shoav six
shok cabbage
shóllivárdo trolley, light cart
shoon to hear
shoshi rabbit
sim to resemble
Siménsa cousin
simmin sauce, gravy, soup
skip basket
skóodalin plate

slang license, summons
slinger dog license
slabérias strawberries
smowrélias raspberries
snaff, shiv snow
snokrel swede
sólivárdo trolley
sónnakai gold
sónnasáster copper; bronze
sootti sleep
sor all
spíngarus skewer
spishi honey
splogger to shoot
stagni nanny-goat
stardi hat
starni deer
stíggerus, stúggerus, stéggus gate
stíraben, stúraben prison, gaol
stoggers, stoggrus stack
stook handkerchief
stor four
strangli, strangler onion
summa stink
swiggler pipe
Ta and
desh ta yek, eleven
táchiben truth
tarder to pull
tarno, tauno, tauni young
tatcho real, true
tatti hot
táttikovi pepper
táttipáni spirits
táttitátti baked potato
tem countryside
grígatem, heath

tiffi sailor
tikni, tikno, titno baby
tit old mare recently in foal
titlaméngro snare
tober road
togs clothes
togram clothes-peg
tompad, tonpad parson
tood milk
tool to hold
toot brass
toov, tuv tobacco
toovlil cigarette paper
tóovalo cigarette, a smoke
totting, tatting rag and bone dealing
tovar axe
trash fright, fear
trashd frightened, afraid
trin three
trindesh, trinanda thirty
trushul about; trail; cross
tukali friendly
tulla fat
tullaben butter
tushni basket
tutóoti, tooti you
tuv tobacco; to smoke
twilers trousers
valin bottle
vardo, wardo caravan, trolley, wagon, cart, covered vehicle
vast hand
wafti, wafeti bad
wardis playing cards
wast hand
wavver other
wel to happen

wélgora a fair; market
wesh, besh, bos forest, wood-
land, copse
weshéngro gamekeeper
weshjook fox
wéshimúlo owl
wiffler pigeon
wongur coal; money
wóngustrin ring on finger

woodrus bed
wooshter to throw
yak, yeck one
yéckorus once
year, yurr ear
yog fire
yogéngri, yogger gun
yogéstowásto tongs
yora, yoro, yaras egg, eggs